LOVE, PAMELA

PAMELA
ANDERSON

DEYST.

An Imprint of WILLIAM MORROW

DEYST.

FOR MY BOYS,

The ones who encouraged me
to write my story
in my
imperfect style.
It's the only way to endure
and describe
my life.
My unique madness,
my legacy.
From my invincible heart alone,
unfiltered.

Love is so short,
and forgetting is so long.

—PABLO NERUDA

LOVE, PAMELA

The lines blur
between dreams
and reality,
or where I end
and the world begins.
To live
and dream
is a wicked dance.
My dreams often come true—
A curse,
and a blessing.

Now that
I've come full circle
I finally feel "safe."
I've stumbled upon a kind of love
that will sustain me—
not only a practical,
friendly,
and compassionate love,

A romance
full of fairies,
nymphs,
and magic.
A true love story—
The love
of self.

More likely,
A tender forgiveness.

Good habits
are hard to recognize
in the context
of all my past
and present decisions.
There is no right
or wrong,
just personal fixations
based on one's history,
trauma,
innocence,
and education.
I was always told I was
"unmanageable."
Nobody agreed with my choices
Maybe
that's a good sign.
I was on no path but my own.

I was a hands-on parent,
No nannies,
The boys'
baseball game schedules
written into my film
and TV contracts.
My children always came first—
no matter what—
Nobody can take that away
from us.

A rarity in Hollywood.

I was
and still am
an exceptionally
easy target.
And,
I'm proud of that.
My defenses are weak.
I'm not bitter,
I don't have the craving to be hard,
heard, or taken seriously.
I prefer
To be fluid
and free,
without boundaries.
Leaving life to chance
and destiny.

"Give me something else I can't handle,"
I'd say—
Up for the challenge.

Life is a series of problems
we must navigate
with grace—
one problem solved,
another arises,
Again
and again
until we die.
I bumble along
pushing those closest to me
to new,
annoying,
and inspiring places,
asking of others
only what I demand
of myself—

I'm
a little girl born
of eccentrically beautiful,
creatively codependent,
unapologetic women,
Who were much too good
for any man.

A collective mermaid society,
Living in sandcastles,
dreaming under seaweed duvets,
oyster shells for dinnerware . . .

My mentors were fierce,
in cotton candy bouffants,
sturdy and wise,
yet weirdly fantastic.
I have been fortunate
to have the feminine wild spirit
whimsical and ever-present
swirling around me,
From my
bombshell mother
to the unique women
who raised her.
Rebel beauties
in Philip Treacy berets,
bent with blue water tactics,
sassy secret weapons.
Tried and true behaviors,
harmlessly loving
and unabashedly
sexy.
A sensuality
armed with
fantastic family recipes,

love, and seduction.
"The way to all men's hearts
is through their stomachs,"
and also,
their starving minds.

I was taught
to never give up
Or relinquish "the chase"—
"Keep it interesting,"
"Don't be too easy"—
To be such a girl these days
Has the opposite signal.
Taboo,
frustrating, unpatriotic,
or problematic.

It is natural
and interesting to me
to blend feminism
and femininity:
Learning the art of the tease
while holding dear
the value of self-worth
right alongside it.
All of this
ingrained in me,
celestial and
genetically loaded.

My memories
seem to be in a blender,
a blur of time,
Decades of delusion,
Confusion.
I prefer not to write about dates,
or years or months
or weeks—
It feels superficial.

The relationships
I've had
are not my life's work—
Well . . .
They are a timeline.

In fact,
I think of my life
not in years,
but by who I was in love with
at that time.
A fuzzy memory.
I call it "soft vision"
like how I look to the camera—
Looking "through" it—
Even past it—
Never
a direct stare to the lens
but a softened focus.

A delicate squint into the abyss
like I could see something further
But not quite make it out.
Curious—
An energy calling me—
Gravity pulling me toward.

Every cover
Every photograph
from my end was literally
a blur.
(It also could've meant I needed glasses.)

Most people's lives go
unrecorded,
or worse,
unlived.
It's quite therapeutic going through
The archives.
I've survived
It's almost like I lived my life
to write about it.

So,
I'm reaching
from here—
Into the deep mud puddle
I've created—
fishing out rocks—

And pulling up the dirtiness
that defends the bottom's
often challenged
depth . . .

That's me—

I devour books and art—
They shape me.
A lump of clay
waiting to be sculpted.
I pour
all I can into me
and
wake up
a new person every day—
achy, ravenous,
and reaching for the watering can.

Though this is a serious book
about abuse,
struggle,
and overcoming,
I hope it is also
Entertaining . . .
and,
more importantly,
Empowering.

My story
might resonate—
a small-town girl
who somehow got tangled up
in her own dream.
Realizing quickly
she had created something
out of nothing.

I lit the fuse
and
It took off without me
like a wild firecracker you can't catch—
whipping playfully,
dangerously unpredictable,
and too hot to handle.
An endless smoking burn—

There were
hardships,
and joy,
And
throughout it all,
I felt led through:
All I needed was
Courage
to take another step—
Knowing
I had angels by my side.
The only protection

I needed,
Along with a firm sense of self.
I have an
unwavering faith in something—
A God,
there has to be—

There was a turning point
when I felt free
to be myself
and not just exist in survival mode—
Liberation—
when I realized
I was my own worst critic,
I decided
to shed the paralyzing shyness
that I was imprisoned by—
Realizing
that life is happening
with
or without me.
A
mindset:
If others can be it,
So can I.

To the young girls
and boys
out there
who are painting their own lives,

"Winging it,"
You're not crazy.
You're brave like me.
Independent thinking and
Disobedience
are important—
And,
you are going to be okay.
I wish someone told me that.
And if they did
I wish
I believed them.

I became a warrior,
A destroyer
of old beliefs,
Slaying dragons.
I embraced
the illuminating thought:
I am "good enough."
I am powerful—

Oh am I . . .

I

I picture myself at 5 years old—
In detail—
I look at her from head to toe—
I watch her for a while
playing,
animated, ludic, theatric—
though on the beach alone.
I call her name to get her attention—
She takes a moment to recognize me
and then runs to me
with open arms.
I hug her tight
and swing her around,
while she smiles her electric smile
and giggles
with innocent
wonder.
I tell her how much I love her,
How beautiful she is,
a wildflower,

and that I'm here for her,
And that
she's going to be okay.
That she's going to get through it all
with flying colors—
I kiss her strong on her sandy cheek—
She smushes up her face
and
wriggles away from me.
Off she runs
in her worn-out
apple-green
terry cloth bikini—
That's trying hard to stay in the places
it is meant to.
She blows me kisses
and waves—
She hurries back to what's important—
Mr. and Mrs. Crab
and
their jellyfish children.

The real me—
unpolluted.

I WAS BORN IN 1967, THE SUMMER OF LOVE. A CENTENNIAL BABY, arriving a healthy seven pounds, seven ounces, on Canada's one hundredth birthday. A hundred years of what, exactly? A manipulated history. Vancouver Island was formed by a volcano 150 million years ago, and First Nations people lived there thousands of years before Columbus set foot on the island. You can't "discover" a land where people already live. History is often rewritten to create heroes out of monsters. Or vice versa. The truth always comes to the surface, eventually.

Will-o'-the-wisp . . .

My parents were young to have me, my mother only seventeen and my dad nineteen. They met in early spring under a big blossoming cherry tree, just in front of the church my mom's family attended most Sundays. She was sitting on the lowest branch, swinging her pretty legs in bobby socks, so the story goes, when Dad and his friend walked by. Dad zeroed in on her and gave his best buddy a quarter to get lost. *Hey, angel,* he said, leaning his arm against the trunk, slicked-back hair and ocean eyes. She was smitten. They immediately fell madly in love. A lightning bolt. *Coup de foudre.*

Their romance was like a 1950s movie. Think *American Graffiti.* Drive-ins, hot rods, burgers split at the local Wings Café. Dad wrote poetry to her on long scrolls of paper lifted from the smelly Crofton paper mill, where he'd worked for a time. He'd write my mom every day, and she'd run to the mailbox after school to get his letters. Even though they lived only a few miles away from each other, it was too far and too long to be apart.

Ladysmith is an old coal-mining town, a place of abandoned sawmills. A fishing village proud with beaches, parks, and First Nations reserves. Not much to do but gossip. Or be gossiped about. My parents were hot trouble, the local Bonnie and Clyde. They were both ridiculously jealous and seemed to enjoy fighting as much as making up. My dad would sneak my underage mom into the local bar—and when the cops came, off they went running, my mom hiding in the bathroom, her bright yellow jumper giving her away. A stern "go home" is all they would get, sometimes a $5 fine.

Dad liked street racing and ended up crashing a few of his cars, most famously a convertible Austin-Healey, which went careening off a small bridge into the sticky spit at Saltair. His reputation is a local mythology, and to this day, everyone has a memory to share: at the grocery store, the liquor store, any store. *Oh, your dad . . . I could tell you stories . . .* I have to stop them and say, *I've heard enough, trust me, but thank you.* They walk away after that with an "oh boy" look, shaking heads. Then a naughty smile, flashing back to the good ol' days, a sudden spring in their step—like they're going to go home to make love to their wives after a long while.

Once, when Dad was trying to outrun the police, he totaled his green Ford Fairlane. Mom was in the passenger seat begging for him to slow down. Her pretty head went through the windshield, the soft cream interior soaked in blood. She was pregnant with me at the time, and we've joked that "that might explain things" (about me, not my mom). She still covers with her hair a long, deep diagonal scar that runs across her forehead from her hairline into her eyebrow.

Their shotgun wedding was modest. I was born a handful of months later, in the local Ladysmith hospital. My dad was out playing cards with the guys, having a few drinks, and missed the birth. Six months later, a photo ran on the front page of the *Ladysmith Chronicle,* my dad holding the "Centennial Baby" medallion, and me on my mother's lap. Kumari-esque.

Our little family lived at Arcady Auto Court, my grandparents' property of nine tiny cabins, nestled in the forest right on the beach. Cabin 6 was ours, set on a grassy knoll, with an ocean view peeking through the ancient arbutus. Though most people around were rough-mouthed and ready, my grandmother had such grace—tall, with perfectly coiffed dark hair and pale skin. She wore chic one-color outfits, lime-green pants and tops cut at the shoulder, and pretty ballet flats. Red nails and lips. A glass of sherry was her breakfast, poured at the Frank Sinatra–style bar full of crystal bottles atop the old cherry Weber piano. Later Grandma rented out the cabins to bikers, mostly. She seemed to like and trust the Hells Angels, too. After Grandpa passed away, I think it made her feel safer to have strong men around who adored her, appreciated her generosity, and would do anything for her. "Acid Eddy's" cabin still stands, and legend has it that there's gold buried somewhere, and possibly a few bodies. I can still remember the sound of bikes intermingling with little birds' chirping, owls' hooting . . . the screeches of eagles.

Wildness
amongst wilderness.

The Auto Court's small store carried the necessities, the staples. Its pink and black lacquered shelves were lined with cigarettes, candy, and newspapers. The fridge was filled with pop, the freezer full of freezies. I would open the lid and lean in headfirst, almost falling in, feet ferociously bicycling, while reaching down into the icy cold to grab my favorite Popsicle. It had to be orange, it was my go-to. You could tell by my swollen, orange-stained lips—the lips I eventually grew into but was teased about as a kid. Grandma would see me and give me that look of "What have you been into?," knowing quite well the answer. I'd look down sheepishly, then smile, orange from nose to chin, and ask her to put my bounty on our "tab," not knowing what that was or that my dad had to pay it off monthly. She'd grab my arm and pull me to the sink, taking a worn-down bar of soap and washing my little hands between hers under the warm sudsy water. Then she'd use an old wrinkly dishcloth, smelling of something strangely antiseptic, to wipe my mouth and send me on my way.

My brother, Gerry, came four years after me, a towhead full of blond curls and with blue eyes, like my mom. A cherub. The opposite of me in every way. I thought Gerry was the most beautiful thing I'd ever seen. He was born July 31, a special local holiday. Another newspaper mention. Another medal.

When my mom was very pregnant with Gerry, we moved down the beach to a three-room cabin on Woodley Road. The shingled roof matched the faded cedar siding and was a driftwood gray from the sea's endless battering and the wet weather. In the winter, icicles hung so low they touched the ground, like a frozen waterfall. The outdoor front porch was part of our living space, with our washing machine and freezer on it, and cases of empty beer bottles, ready to be taken to the bottle depot on the weekends.

The cabin was steps to the sand. I was good at running across barnacles barefoot, sprinting over them like they were hot coals. I'm not sure my feet even touched the jagged shells. The pebbly sand, rocks, crabs, tide pools, starfish: a wonderland of rich and healthy sea life on our doorstep. My playground.

My world was the ocean.
And I always had a toe in it.

Our home was small. There wasn't much room for all of us at once, so Gerry and I played outside mostly, even in the rain. I always felt safer outdoors than in. I loved climbing the three-tiered rock garden behind the house, full of wild poppies, peonies, and blackberry bushes . . . We slid around in puddles, picking wildflowers and berries, and occasionally stole a few precious "don't touch my" daffodils from Mom's garden. My favorite spaces were surrounded by fragrant purple lilacs, sour grapes in vines strangling the trunks of tart green apple trees. Gerry and I would make mud pies, and I'd set a "table" with sticks and leaves in the dirt, placing our stolen flowers in the middle. Then we'd eat the pies—a little bit of dirt never hurt anyone.

My mom gave us
everything
and my dad's love was
different—
clever, genius,
always slightly angry,
but mostly frustrated with himself
I think.
Love is what saved him.
They were the missing pieces of each other—

My shining example—
What I've aspired to
my whole human life
Unfortunately
and fortunately—

My model of love
is slightly screwed
not only
skewed—

And,
hard to live up to—

My mother was everything to me, so funny and beautiful, the bright center of our lives. We were all so in love with her, me, Gerry, my dad. She was petite, a bouncy, giggly blonde. Not near stupid, but naïve. I can see her clearly, waving her white silk scarf, playing surrender, acting helpless to the camera, batting the biggest blue eyes you've ever seen. Just a knockout. Two dresses hung on the line among our grubby underwear and socks—one with buttery yellow flowers to match her hair, the other bright turquoise blue to match her eyes. She wore her hair in a cute blond bouffant, tinted a pinky or lilac pastel, and would tell stories of how, when she was younger, she would use soup cans to roll up her hair. She and her girlfriends would share the soup, then rinse out the cans for their collection. They couldn't always afford to eat well, but they could always afford to be beautiful. *There's no excuse not to look good,* she would say. Her hair never suffered, even if she had to.

My dad also had great style, an undeniable swagger. He'd wear white T-shirts with a pack of menthol Camel cigarettes tucked in the sleeve. Always a watch on his left wrist, the face on the inside. He wore his dark hair slicked back in a ducktail just like Elvis, though he was maybe better-looking. Ever the notorious "bad boy." Both my parents carried a natural glamour despite their rough wildness, though they were too young to carry it off entirely.

My dad was a reader, a thinker, a dreamer. Still a trouble-maker. Always questioning. In school, he was a straight-A student. The lawyer among friends, he would argue anything. He studied Latin; he read the Bible ten times. He'd question teachers to the point of distraction and was sent home for voicing his beliefs, always challenging the status quo, playfully demanding that if it was anyone, it was Eric the Red who "discovered" America.

I was taught to question authority—
and so I question everything.

My grandpa Herman was an original thinker, too. A rogue scholar. He was a romantic, an anonymous poet for the *Lady-smith Chronicle,* a spiritual docent. Grandpa had been a logger his entire life, the wild one who danced on hundred-foot tree-tops. I picture him leaning back in his green leather La-Z-Boy, book in hand, while my grandmother sat nearby listening closely to her police scanner, always keeping up on the local gossip. Grandpa would read to me from *Bulfinch's Mythology,* in a voice deeper than Barry White's. He also taught me how to speak Finnish. I carried a little Finnish dictionary with me everywhere, learning new words and sentences to try to impress him. We liked that we could speak in front of others and they wouldn't understand.

When I asked Grandpa what religion I was, he told me I was agnostic. I thought he meant "antagonistic" and would tell people that—to quizzical looks—for a long while. After some age and research, I realized that he meant nothing with God could be known or not known, neither faith nor disbelief. My spirituality was up to me. Nobody told me what to believe—I would find God in my own way. Or not. I was raised in a way where nobody was telling me what to do or how to be, or how to think, or what to believe, and I'm eternally grateful for that. It's the ultimate gift. Grandpa's strong connection to and deep respect for nature was a profound legacy. He was the one who convinced me that elves and fairies exist, that the trees can talk to us and to each other. That if you place little mirrors in the garden, you can catch a fairy's reflection. And don't doubt me, I have seen them with my own eyes.

We didn't have much growing up, but Mom was a magical mood setter. She'd leave trails of flower petals and notes around the house, and homemade surprises for Christmas, Easter, Valentine's Day . . . She never missed a holiday, with little gifts for us or my dad, whatever she could afford. She worked a few jobs—waitressing, picking strawberries, digging clams, selling vacuum cleaners—while my dad was mostly a chimney sweep who set his own hours. Every night, she had dinner on the table at five P.M. It was something we depended on, and I realize now how important that was to Gerry and me, that routine and consistency, even if they were TV dinners. My favorite was macaroni with a can of stewed tomatoes, and I still crave Mom's pierogies—minus the bacon—and canned beets.

If Mom was exhausted, she didn't show it. I always wanted to make her laugh, realized from a young age that I loved to see her smile. I'd come sliding out of my room in my mom's Velcro rollers, acting out the Enjoli perfume commercial—*I can bring home the bacon, fry it up in a pan . . . never let you forget you're a man—*

'cause I'm a woman—and then run back. We had no door to our room, so I'd stop quickly and cozy up to the doorframe and listen intently for my parents' laughter, proud of myself, quietly giggling. Then I'd plan my next performance.

My mom also did silly things that cracked her up and made us laugh, too. Goofy calisthenics and stretching, jumping jacks, and my favorite—the "bum walk" across the yard, a little maneuver where you sit on the ground, legs in front of you, and scoot forward on your bum. Mom would do this "workout" with a few friends—all glam ladies in cute cardigans who had the same beehive hairstyle, but in different colors—laughing the whole way. Mom was funny, Lucille Ball funny.

My mom always said there is no such thing as natural beauty—it takes at least an hour in front of a mirror—and you are more powerful if you are pretty. As a complete contrast to my mom's effortful beauty—hair perfectly set, in a crisp T-shirt and jeans rolled up, cute gardening gloves—I was a tomboy. I would play with anything that creeped or crawled: a slow daddy longlegs picking its way across the ground, safe because they can't bite you with those long legs; a slithery garter snake I could carry around; even bees, which fascinated me—so much so, I was once stung over and over inspecting a nest. Another time, I grabbed a big beach rat by its tail, and the rat ran off while I still had the tail in my hand. I pulled it right out of its bum somehow. I felt terrible but was amazed and showed it off. It was easy to make my mom and her friends scream.

I had a ton of energy spilling out of me all the time and not a lot of places to use it. We didn't have the money for after-school stuff, but I always found a way. Figure skating was expensive. I rented skates and got myself into the local Ice Capades. I was one of the dalmatians in *101 Dalmatians* (minus ninety-five, so six of us in dalmatian costumes). My mom used shoe polish to blacken one of my eyes, but it stung and smeared into black tears. We went onto the ice, pumping along, holding on to each other's waists, but I couldn't see and tripped, taking the whole line of dogs down with me.

There was a free community acrobatics class, where they called me "rubber band," because I could do the splits all three ways and could do twenty back walkovers in one spot and not move. Since I was so small, I'd be the one they tossed from pyramid to pyramid. I loved the way it felt when I was in the air—like I was weightless, like anything could happen. I was tempting death and knew at a very young age that I had unwavering courage.

The piano lessons I took were through a family friend. The Suzuki method involves learning by ear—my teacher would play, then I would mimic her. I was good at it. Music was always in our house. My parents played a lot of country music, and I'd sing along to George Strait and Elvis (*So dreamy*, my mom would say), or to Tammy Wynette's "I Don't Wanna Play House" with my mom while it played on the record player. She'd be swinging her hips, washing the dishes, while I'd be dancing around her, singing, *I don't wanna play house; it makes my mommy cry.*

Mom would take me to the drive-in with her friends. Everyone smoked—I hated how it burned my eyes, while they gossiped and puffed on one cigarette after the other. *You're not going to tell your father any of this, you hear me?* she'd say, sprinkling me with a handful of popcorn. I wasn't sure what the big secret was—the fact that we were spending money on junk food, or the Elvis movie they were swooning over—but I agreed while choking on smoke, rubbing my eyes, just trying to survive in the back seat.

When Mom was at work, that's when the real fun began. My dad would take us along when he went to play poker with his friends. We'd go off-roading through the woods, bouncing around in the back of his clay-green Land Rover. Falling all over, without seat belts, laughing and bumping our heads, hysterical as we drove over logs and through ditches. Up steep hills, screaming, scared we were going to tip over backward. *Don't tell your mom.* We would drive to Regan's Pool—an abandoned and empty pool covered in graffiti in the middle of the forest—where he and his friends played cards and drank. Dad's close friends liked for us to call them "uncle." There was Uncle Grift (self-explanatory). Uncle Leo, my dad's best friend, who helped him trim the trees by shooting the "widow-maker" branches off with their trusty shotguns. And then there was Uncle Lem, a feisty, loudmouthed logger who had a mail-order bride. And when she learned English, she left him and stole the toaster. He owed my dad $500 and was on the run until he died. Dad's still mad he never got it back. They'd bring coolers full of beer, and it was the kids' job to make sure they never ran out. We'd run back and forth from the cooler, high-speed waiters. I had the coveted job of holding the opener. They had to come to me first to open the bottles—I was powerful. I would be covered in beer suds that I licked off my arms. It was a messy job.

DAD PLAYED PIANO AND PARTIED A LITTLE LIKE JERRY LEE LEWIS. He would take out the accordion and the spoons as the violet sun started setting. "Green Door" was a favorite. *What's that secret you're keeping . . .* Once the beer came out, with oysters shucked and swallowed straight off the beach, Mom would dance, twisting away to a melody I think only she could hear.

I remember seminude clambakes, a black cast-iron pot fitted in the sand on top of a fire, clams popping, steamed in beer and butter. Skinny-dipping late nights in an ocean full of jellyfish, splashing gently, laughing, the phosphorescence in the cold black water, bonfires blazing on the beach. Pretty girls squealing in nothing but brassieres and high-waisted shorts, taunting the boys from the water's edge. Lanky men in soggy, stretched-out underpants howling at the moon. Along with our dog, Lobo, who was part wolf.

The next morning, Gerry and I would set up chairs over the men who were still passed out on the deck and flick rocks at their heads. We turned it into a game, and got chased and cursed at for it, but could always outrun the hangovers.

It still makes me uncomfortable to see
a grown man stumble,
And I've seen a few . . .

Dad's younger sister, Auntie Sherry, drove a blue Stingray Corvette and had the most beautiful handwriting on earth, a bubbly script. I wanted to emulate her in every way. His older sister was my auntie Marlene. She was deaf and called me "Bappely." She read lips, just maybe not that well. At that time, there were few resources for deaf people, so she kept her own ways of listening and communicating. When I visited her, we would have tea. When she'd look away, I'd cheekily move the teapot slightly to see if she'd notice. She'd move it back. Then

I'd nudge the sugar ever so slightly. She'd move it back, placing it exactly as she'd had it, with a sigh.

Auntie Marlene took care of all the feral cats near her house. I could tell she had a special language with animals. They followed her like she was a pied piper. I studied Auntie Marlene with curiosity, wanting to learn her secrets. I too had an affinity with animals and had learned to trust them more than people. I collected misfits—like an orange tabby cat that walked sideways and an abandoned baby bobcat. I was the one you brought the birds with the broken wings to. The ones nobody else wanted or had the patience for.

Dad liked to go hunting with his friends. I remember dead animals tied to the hoods of trucks and guns hanging on the wall. There was a story of how one time a deer they'd shot got up and ran away, right when the guys posed for photos next to their kill, all their rifles placed in the dead deer's antlers. They laughed maniacally about it. Dad would fill the crusty yellow freezer on our porch with venison and moose meat wrapped in brown, bloodstained paper. I'd call it "funny meat," because it tasted strange, a gamey wildness to it. It just felt wrong to eat it.

Dad told me never to go inside the pump house, so, of course, it was all I wanted to do. I'd stare out at it in our backyard and imagine all sorts of things happening inside . . . but I never could've dreamed up what was actually in there. Finally, one day I mustered the courage, and when no one was looking, I sneakily broke through the fence and opened the creaky door to see a headless deer hanging upside down. A large muscular body, dripping blood into a bucket. I stood frozen, admiring and screaming at the same time. My eyes fell on the severed head sitting next to the body on a bloody stump. I took in the big, dead eyes, dark and deep, rimmed by thick lashes. They seemed to stare back at me and pierce my soul in its profoundest fluttering vulnerability. That was meat? I'd never forgive my parents.

That turned me off eating animals and turned me into an activist. I was around six or seven years old, and I thought: It's not fair, animals have no gun, no voice. Maybe I could be their voice. I convinced Dad to never hunt again by inflicting as much emotional trauma on him as I could. I made him sorry till my pigtails stood on end, fountaining tears, begging him. He promised me he'd never hunt again, and he didn't. I recognized what little power I had. It was a start.

Like all children
I had a naïve understanding—
that what was said was true—
what I read was true—
what was told to me was true—
Lying
was not something
I understood—
yet.

AT A YOUNG AGE, I LEARNED THAT PEOPLE ARE MOSTLY AWFUL. Babysitters even worse.

That's what happens when you are inappropriately messed with as a child. In my case, it was a young female babysitter who sexualized me very early, forcing me to play weird games on her body, like "car." She'd bring me used toys—like a life-size Barbie head where I could style the hair and put makeup on the face. My parents thought she was generous and kind, when really, it was just a way to get them off the scent. At the time, I couldn't understand any of it. She threatened me and told me not to tell anyone. Or else.

Why were people so awful, and what was I going to do about it? My parents were honest with me—honest to a fault—but when someone asked me not to say something, it hurt me to the core.

I was innocent
an acrobat,
a gymnast,
a double-jointed tomboy
with an endless imagination.
Furiously building sandcastles
at tremendous speed
Creating my own world as fast as I could.

WE HAD FEW NEIGHBORS ON WOODLEY ROAD, BUT LUCKILY, WE lived next door to the Atkinson family, whose home was a sanctuary for me. I would show up at their house every day, like their fourth child. I had crazy crushes on the two older brothers, Matt and John, and would write them anonymous love letters in crayon that only could have been from me. Their sister Sara was closer to my age. She took dance lessons—ballet, jazz, tap—and I would hang around their house, waiting for her to get home. She'd show up wearing her pretty leotard and teach me a few steps. Me in my jean cutoffs and dirty T-shirt . . . shuffle ball change.

Mrs. Atkinson was a stay-at-home mom, while Mr. Atkinson was a successful businessman who owned the cable company that supplied the TV stations to the island. He was a mentor to many, I've come to find out, and I was blessed to be someone this family took an interest in and cared for when I needed it most. It was a different world. I never even knew what a salad was until I saw one at Sara's house. Her mother must have asked me to get her something, because I never would have opened someone else's refrigerator on my own—I'd never have been that impolite. I remember taking in the bountiful shelves of the refrigerator, in stark contrast to my own, and my eyes landing on a big wooden bowl with mushrooms carefully placed around the edges, cucumber in the next ring, then grated carrots and chopped red onions in the middle. It was art, this mandala spinning in front of me. I stared at it for a very long time, too long for a fridge to be open. I was transfixed till Mrs. Atkinson nudged me gently, saying, *Pamela, darling* . . . She noticed my confusion and was touched, and asked if I wanted to help her prepare dinner more often. And I really wanted to.

I knew that right by their back door, there were dog treats kept on the counter in a big glass jar. I was allowed to take a couple on the way out to give to their pretty German shorthaired pointer, Topey. We would sit side by side on the back porch, holding paws, and eat them together, lost in thought, looking out to the ocean. One for him, one for me.

My parents were always quick to say things like, *If only we had money, things would be better.* But I already knew then that it would take much more than that.

THINGS WERE HEATING UP AT HOME. DAD SENT MOM'S NEW ELEC-
trolux vacuum flying over her head. It went off the deck, down
the bank, over the boathouse, and onto the beach. She had
been trying to tidy the living room, the coffee table full of ash-
trays, the worn brown corduroy couch strewn with Lucky beer
bottles, the local favorite. Hockey blared on the TV. We knew
not to make noise, or else. When he got like this after too many,
Dad would call my mom names. "Dingbat" or "stupid." My
dad was incredibly smart, in Mensa, huge IQ, and when he
got drunk and angry, he always went after Mom's intelligence.
Those words really hurt. Name-calling was something I didn't
like—and I witnessed it far too often.

Times like this, I'd take Gerry outside and sit on the stairs.
When we couldn't hear yelling anymore, we'd assume they had
made up. We would usually walk in on them making out on the
couch, or on the table, or up against the fridge. I'd quickly pull
Gerry by the hand outside again and find something else to do.

They were not like other parents I saw—
Their passion was undeniable,
their fights, the tears
and the yelling—
But somehow it ended up our normal—
Sometimes Gerry and I felt
In the way of their time together
Or that we were the problem.

I remember my mom crying a lot, always quietly in the
bathroom with the door closed. I'd hear her muffled sobs and

could faintly make out that she was talking to herself, trying to calm herself down. We had only the one bathroom, and if you looked through the keyhole, you could see everything. I'd watch Mom trying to tease her hair and fix her makeup, the mascara running down her face. The mirror was on the wall over the toilet, so she had to kneel on the seat to see herself, with her makeup and hairbrushes, lipstick and pale pink teasing comb, splayed out on the back of the tank. I wonder if she knew I was watching.

My beautiful sad mom
Made me a melancholy child
She was a living Mel Ramos Keyhole painting.

I'd go into the bathroom and stand on the toilet seat to look at myself like she did, combing my hair, trying on her pale pink lipstick. Even as a child, I hated the way I looked. I was always small for my age, lean and athletic. One time I noticed the mirror opened—it was a hidden medicine cabinet. I saw a bottle of pink pills. Chewable baby aspirin. They looked like candy, so I ate them all. Next thing I knew, I was in the hospital. It wasn't the first time. I'd been to the hospital plenty in my short life—I was an orange baby, had walking pneumonia, and "bent a bone" and ended up in a cast—but this time Mom was more nervous, afraid they'd take me away from her. And for good reason—some kids we knew had just been taken away from another friend's family the week before. They lived in a hotel room above the local bar. Their mom told us she saw little green people in her plants. I always looked, hoping to see them. We were there when the kids were taken away. I remember waving to them when they drove off with the social workers in a white van. We never saw them again.

When my parents fought, I'd say to myself, à la Winnie the Pooh, *Think, think, think.* Once, I told Gerry to come with me, then instructed him to get into an old cable barrel in the neighbors' yard and not to move. I put the lid on, then I called 911 and reported him missing. The search went on for what seemed like hours, until he emerged, tired of the game. He probably wanted to see the fire trucks and police cars, whose sirens were ringing through the neighborhood. He told everyone that I had told him to stay in there. I knew I was in big trouble, but I had started to get used to the belt. It was worth it; I could take a few licks. God knows it was worse for my mom. It's sad to look back knowing I probably caused her a lot of grief, instigating trouble when she tried to keep things perfect, so Dad wouldn't get mad at her or us. She always tried to cover for him, but Gerry and I weren't stupid. Something wasn't right. We were afraid for our mom. It affected us deeply.

Some nights, I'd pretend to be sleeping while I waited for my parents to go to bed. Then I'd get up quietly—very difficult to do, climbing down our clunky red iron bunk bed—and I'd almost sleepwalk to the kitchen and put the stopper in the sink, turn on the water, and go back to bed, flooding it. Or I'd mix all my mom's spices into the butter. Then butter the cat. My dad was an early riser, and I'd wake up to his yelling, *Pamelaaaaaaaa!* It was an exciting feeling.

One night, my parents went out for a date, but Dad forgot his leather jacket and they came home unexpectedly. My cat Momsy had just given birth to another set of kittens under the washing machine on our deck. I decided to bring them inside, which I'd been told point-blank not to do. Dad walked back in to see me holding the box of kittens. I was horrified, caught red-handed. He was so angry, he threw his jacket down, grabbed a paper bag, stuffed all of the kittens inside, and stumbled down the steps to the beach with them. I followed in a trance—I could hear the kittens' muffled cries. Everything blurred, like it was happening in slow motion. My dad walked into the ocean and held the bag underwater. He drowned them in front of me. I felt like I died that night, too.

It was my fault—
I was bad.
I left my body,
floated to my friend Sara's house.
I imagined flying over the trees,
down the driveway
into her house
around the corner into her room—
into her closet—
closing the door
and sitting with her pretty toys.
A refuge.

I didn't say much to anyone about my home life. It was sensitive, and I innately understood that it was just what we had been dealt. I was grateful for what we had. I could not have survived my adult life without the strength I learned to muster early on.

In school, my teachers praised me for my creativity and inventiveness. I would exert my artistic freedom in unique ways and was a sponge for experience. I loved to write and would get lost in storytelling. I'd feel so inspired that I just *had* to get the words out, saying my pencil came to life and had a mind of its own. Sometimes I'd write about outer space, with drawings to accompany the text, the characters vivid in my mind. I was interested in aliens—I even knew their names. Once, we took a trip to the natural history museum. It set me on fire. The dinosaur bones told me to be an archaeologist. I started to look for fossils and fool's gold on my beach and had quite the collection. I polished rocks in a tumbler and set up a store in a big fallen tree, selling to my pretend customers.

As much as I enjoyed school, I could be an agent provocateur. Sometimes, I'd act like I was deaf during class, or I'd wrap my arm in toilet paper and say I'd broken it, or I'd pretend to fall asleep at my desk, fake snoring, until I started laughing. Once, I cut off my hair in chunks, then wore a K-Way rain jacket over my head and pulled the strings of the hood very tight, so I had only a little hole to look through.

The funny thing was, I was painfully shy in many ways. But I liked the attention on my terms. I didn't have many friends—one-on-one wasn't my strength—but I could perform to a whole classroom. I remember standing up on my desk one day and inviting everyone ice skating, without my parents' knowledge, permission, or ability. I never had friends come to my house—even from a young age, I didn't feel comfortable doing that—but it just felt good, just for a minute, to pretend. Everyone clapped at the end of my speech. I took that in.

By Saturday, I had forgotten all about it, so I was surprised when a girl showed up that day with ice skates around her neck, skipping to the front door, holding her mom's hand. I had to run into the yard to catch them before they got to the door, to say that we couldn't go. My mom was at work and my dad was asleep on the couch. I didn't even make up any excuse. The girl's mom seemed to figure it out and looked at me with sadness, smiling tenderly at me as she took in the surroundings while leading her confused daughter away. They were new in town. Nobody else came—they knew I was "kidding." I felt very small, and I was embarrassed to go back to school. I became more distant, withdrawn. Unsure of my place in the world. Sometimes sitting at my desk, hands on my lap, eyes lowered.

I HAD A SECRET. I WAS DIGGING A HOLE TO CHINA. I WOULD crawl down to a small flat dirt landing that only I could get to, through the blackberry bushes, on my stomach, spoon in hand. I would slide a board over the hole when I was too tired to dig anymore. My mom kept wondering why her spoons were going missing. This started when I had the babysitter who couldn't keep her hands to herself. The last straw was when she tried to tell me that I was a "bad girl" and Santa Claus wasn't coming. I could not accept that—it was winter and I was counting the sleeps till Christmas. I ran after her in tears, calling her a liar . . . and clumsily stabbed her with a candy-cane-striped pen in her chest. I hated her stinky Supertramp T-shirt and ugly big boobs she always stuck in my face. *I hope you die!* I screamed through tears. Then I ran for my life.

Soon after, she died in a car accident. I couldn't tell my parents that I'd killed her with my magical mind, or that she was touching me and making me touch her in ways I don't want to remember. I just forgot about it all, pushed it away and hoped no one would ever find out. I carried that my entire young life. I was very careful about what I wished for from then on.

I eventually gave up on getting to China.
I might only be halfway there anyway
I thought—
It's too far still to go—
My dreams of being an archaeologist
and world traveler
were fading.

I I

I'D LOST COUNT OF HOW MANY TIMES WE'D LEFT MY DAD. WE'D always jump into my mom's beat-up red Honda and run to a girlfriend's house till things settled down, sleeping on their couch for the night. But this time it felt more real. I was told to keep watch, to make sure my dad didn't come and try to steal the car—he'd done that a few times before. High in the tree was my lookout. When he and his friends drove up, I scurried down, scratching myself up, bloodied, and ran inside to tell my mom. She and her girlfriend were playing cards and threw down their hands quickly, running into the street. They were in matching gingham capri pants and no shoes, yelling after the car, *Barryyyyy*. My dad and his buddies thought it was funny. The car fishtailing, beers in hand, a trail of smoke out the window.

As Mom bandaged and cleaned my scrapes, she was talking frantically to her friend about this being the last time . . . She was so upset, this time we were leaving my father "for good." Soon after, we left the island and drove to Kamloops, moving into a welfare apartment across from my mom's sister, Debbie. We lived off food stamps and powdered milk. I'll never forget the chalky taste. I dreaded my cereal in the morning.

Mom looked for work every day, combing the Help Wanted ads in the paper. With a background mainly in waitressing, she had limited choices. And she could leave us alone in the apartment for only so long. She finally got a cleaning job at the hospital. She wore a pale blue uniform and would go straight there when we got home from school. She had awful stories of cleaning the morgue at night—nobody else wanted to do it. She had no fear of hard work, only elevators, so she walked the stairs, carrying her buckets and mops anywhere she went. Her schedule was sporadic, and she had to work on call, sometimes entire nights, which meant, unfortunately, we were left alone, or worse—more babysitters.

Gerry and I were a bit confused, coming from an island. In Kamloops, there was no beach, no ocean, no rocky mountains. It was dry, with hills full of grasshoppers. All we had was a parking lot to play in, where Gerry and I met some local kids. We'd sit on the cars and talk about our dreams. I wanted to be a wild horse, or at least meet one. The other kids wanted remote-control toys, fireworks, and such. Gerry and I called them the "dirty kids." They were sweet but filthy. They were kind, though, and always offered to share their breakfast with us. They'd look at us scrawny kids and ask us, *Wanna hunk of a piece of toast?* They'd rip the bread apart and give us small pieces, and we'd all sit together eating toast on the hood of their black Trans Am with big gold wings painted on it.

Close by, I found a horse ranch and an orchard. I'd climb up the wooden fence and reach over and pick apples, holding as many as I could fit in my scooped-up T-shirt. Then I'd go hang on the ranch fence and feed the horses. My only real pet during this time was a white cat named Sugar, though she wasn't truly ours. We shared her in the community, and when she disappeared one day, nobody would tell me what happened. I never stopped looking for her, posting pictures that I'd drawn all around the neighborhood.

Kamloops is where I started passing out. *Low blood pressure,* said the doctor. They told me that I had exactly four seconds to save myself, wherever I was. If I felt that feeling coming on, I had to quickly lie down and put my feet up a wall, elevated above my heart. This might keep me from fainting. And even if I did, I'd have less distance to fall. They called me "Pass-Out Pam" at school. Once, at the mall with friends, I had to lie down and put my feet up in the middle of the walkway, people stepping over me, oblivious to a kid lying there.

I felt invisible
at times.
Just particles of energy that people
walked through—
I felt like
I had no edges,
no borders to contain me—
melting, spilling everywhere—

We stayed in Kamloops for what felt like a year before Dad found us. He called, and I happened to pick up the phone. He told me he'd been in a car accident, but he was okay and doing better. He wanted to come get us. I wanted him to come get us, too. With my hand covering the receiver, so no one could hear, looking around cautiously, I whispered to my dad that we were in Kamloops, close to Auntie Debbie, reading the exact address off a piece of mail. He said he was on his way. Mom was surprised when he showed up at our door, but underneath the shock was a sense of relief, like she'd been waiting for him all this time. You could see it when they looked at each other, the deep, undeniable love. I remember their embrace. I felt it from across the room. He was the only man she could ever love. And she was his angel.

We moved back to the island, though not to Ladysmith. Mom never wanted to return there—too many bad memories. So we moved up-island to Comox. Dad stopped drinking and wore a round cowboy hat to cover his shaved head from the accident, along with an oval jade bolo tie. He started a new business and got a white truck with BARRY'S FURNACE SERVICE written on the side, along with our phone number: 339-2323. He'd drive me to school and I'd ask him to drop me off on the corner, embarrassed by the run-down, dirty white flatbed, an obvious work truck. The entire drive would be in silence, no talking or anything. I was starting to think I liked my dad better when he drank? This was less interesting, being "normal." I wasn't comfortable being comfortable.

AT SCHOOL, THE OTHER GIRLS WERE DEVELOPING AT A FASTER rate than me. I should've known what was happening, but when I grew a lump on my chest, just on one side, I tried hard to pound it back in. I spent days rehearsing how I'd tell my mom I had cancer. When I finally told her, she laughed and said, *Oh, dolly, you are just becoming a woman!* Oh, I thought. Then the other nipple appeared, and there was no stopping it. I was two nipples walking in the door. I hated to think about them, because when I did, it became worse. They'd burst through any shirt I was wearing. It felt like pliers were pinching and pulling.

I was not what you would call a girly girl. One girlfriend would always ask me if she could put makeup on me and do my hair. The goal was to look "older," and I soon found out why. She had a "friend," an older guy, and we were going to his place. He was maybe twenty. I was much too young to be there—we were only twelve, thirteen? Trying so hard to be grown-up. My mom thought I was going to the movies, because that's where she dropped us off. But when a black Corvette pulled into the parking lot and my friend told me to get in with her, I did. I shouldn't have, but I did. I looked no more than ten years old. Even with makeup, I wouldn't have passed for thirteen. I was barely, if even, a teenager.

At the guy's town house, my friend went upstairs with him, while his roommate said he wanted to teach me to play backgammon. I naïvely said okay. Then he wanted to give me a back rub. Then he forced himself on me. It wasn't hard to get me out of the tube top I was wearing. And no matter how much I tried to fight him off, he was also able to get my shorts down. In the struggle, I lost my tiny "P" necklace, a treasured birthday present from my parents. I was reaching for it when he pierced my body. I screamed with pain and called out for my friend, wanting to leave. I couldn't see, I couldn't breathe, I was blinded by pain. I ran and locked myself in the bathroom to inspect what had happened to me—there was blood and other stuff . . . I felt sick as I cleaned myself up, trying to get it together.

The lost necklace didn't get by my mom, who looked at me quizzically when she picked us up back at the movie theater.

Little did she know that wasn't the only thing that had been lost. I was no longer a virgin. Forced, against my will.

I didn't tell anybody.
I didn't tell anybody.
I was in shock,
falling apart, molecules, dust, liquid . . .
My life evaporating

After, I thought everyone could tell—like I had it tattooed on my forehead. I was sure I looked different. I thought I was bad, and I was ashamed. It hurt me a lot, keeping this secret. It was so confusing, and I didn't know who to go to. I knew I shouldn't have been there, and I didn't want to get anyone in trouble. I started to trust the people around me even less. Eventually, I just blocked it out.

I tried to keep myself busy at school. Being a good student was something I took seriously. I was very organized and would complete all my assignments on time. I rewrote my notebooks and edited my binders, to keep them looking neat and tidy. I was an overachiever. I played volleyball on the senior team, even though I was a junior, and was athlete of the year. I looked like a little boy compared to my peers, and especially the girls on my team. Though I did get the "golden buns" award at volleyball camp, unexpectedly.

My dad convinced me to play saxophone in band and take chorus. It was an outlet. I found I enjoyed singing and was asked to sing soprano, jazz, and even the scat solos sometimes. *Scooby dootin', doobie dootin', doo, dot doot dow . . . ba dootin' doo wah, ba dootin' doo wahhhh.*

I had one serious boyfriend through high school. His nickname was Boogieman Jack. We were always making out, kissing or fighting. He was handsome, a bad boy, a hot rod enthusiast with a hot temper. I loved his family even more than I loved him. His mom was an amazing cook, who made me a cookbook of her favorite Ukrainian recipes. I was always interested in cooking. My mom could set a pretty table and bake for days, but family meals were fast and on a budget. I started cooking for myself as soon as I was able. The meals I liked to make were clean and pretty on a plate, a roasted carrot with sprig of rosemary from the garden, a jam jar of wildflowers, and homemade lemonade with lavender ice cubes.

Jack worked at a garage as an apprentice mechanic, so he was one of the first boys I knew with a car. He drove a Buick 225—"Deuce and a Quarter"—with dingle balls and fuzzy dice, lowered with hydraulics so it bounced to the music, heavy on the subwoofers. We would drive around, listening to Cheap Trick's "I Want You to Want Me." One angry night, he started kicking me over and over, until he physically kicked me out of his car while he was driving. He pushed me with his foot so hard, I had no choice but to open the door when the car was moving and rolled straight into a ditch. Mind you, I landed a perfect gymnast dismount, at high speed. I ran home as fast as I could, luckily only a few blocks away. A neighbor noticed and ran after me to my door to see that I was okay.

My dad always waited up when I was out. I had run straight by him to get to my bedroom unnoticed. But after speaking to the neighbor, he came pounding on my door and was about to kick it in when I finally opened it. I didn't look too good. I was a mess, trying to hide my tears. He took one glance at me and, without a word, pulled me out of my room, put me in his truck, and drove us to Jack's house. It was late, but Dad went right inside without knocking and grabbed Jack from his bedroom and took him outside. Dad pinned that bugger up against a wall. From where I was, I could only see his feet dangling. Words were exchanged. My dad said nothing when he got back to the car. I was embarrassed more than anything.

As I matured, I noticed most of my boyfriends were bad— and progressively got worse. I often wondered *why*. Did I turn them into assholes? Was I doing something wrong? Did I make them crazy? They would turn violent, mean, cruel, so quickly. I felt I did everything to try to get them to love me, by being accommodating, generous, or by just being the comedian— laughter always being an easy way for me to cut the tension.

I tend to see diamonds
in lumps of coal—
gold
in nickel—
I'm an
alchemist.
Luring in
these fantastical characters
who would consistently
undo me.

Jack and I were on and off all through high school and slightly beyond. Each time he wanted me back, I caved. I always thought maybe this time he might turn into Prince Charming. But he was jealous, and he would get mean: If he heard me singing, he'd say I was tone-deaf. If we were dancing, he'd say I had no rhythm. Those little things were meant to try to erode my confidence—and to an extent, they did. I believed him and stopped, making me question my abilities, the things I loved, the things that made me happy. I broke up with Jack over and over, but he wouldn't go away.

Then one day, a new boy appeared. Leaning on my locker, confident, different—very few new kids came to the school. Billy might not have been as tall as Jack, but he was . . . cute. He had just moved to Comox from a big city. He was in a gang and could use nunchakus. I was impressed and thought he'd be good security, because I was still afraid of my last boyfriend. But Billy was his own kind of bad boy. I remember him hiding me in the back seat of his souped-up muscle car under a blanket with a Coke Slurpee from the local gas station while he and his friends went to collect money from someone. They were successful, I guess, and came back all fired up. They held me down, pulled my shirt up, and put hickeys all over me. And it got worse—there were at least four, maybe six boys—I blacked out.

I was starting to lose faith
in everyone.
What little I had.

In high school, I was only five foot two (I grew five inches after high school). And I weighed less than a hundred pounds till I was in my twenties, when my curves naturally formed. I did not start my menstrual cycle till I was eighteen. After high school, I thought I'd never get it. So the "incidents" were never a pregnancy worry. But I was definitely stunted. Some say because I was so athletic. Others say because of trauma.

It was unbearable for me.

I tried to go on as if nothing had happened, hanging out with friends more. I remember a party at the PMQs (Private Military Quarters) at the US Air Force base. The guys were behaving badly, like frat boys. I was not impressed. I heard a cat screeching bloody murder from the kitchen and ran in to find these assholes trying to fry a cat in a cast-iron frying pan. I grabbed the cat, who was hissing and scared, wrapped him in my sweater, and fled to another room, where I called my dad to pick me up. Dad and I had a deal: I would never be in trouble if I told him the truth, and I was never to get in a car with someone who was drinking. He would come anywhere, anytime, to drive my friends and me home. And he always did. So I called him and said I'd found a "kitten" and asked if I could take him home. Dad sounded grumpy but said yes for now. He laughed when he saw me. *By the way, that's no kitten.* Sneakers was full grown but skinny—he lived another twenty years, fat and happy. And was my dad's best friend, even if he didn't want to admit it.

GERRY WAS STARTING TO GET INTO THAT SMALL-TOWN KIND OF trouble. Scrappy, rebellious, partying with friends. One night he overdosed. I was hysterical when I got to the hospital, angry that his friend wouldn't tell me what he had taken. I was furious with that punk—he wouldn't talk, just mumbled something incoherent. I screamed, *Tell me now, you little shit! What has he taken? What did you give him?* I went wild, kicking that rotten kid with all my might down the emergency hall, over and over, in his rear end. I had to blame someone else. The nurses had to hold me back.

It took me some time to calm down, and when I did, I had to recognize that, even with the anger, I was grateful that the kid had gotten Gerry to the hospital. He saved my brother's life, most likely. I knew deep down that Gerry was responsible for himself, I just couldn't bear the thought of losing him.

My mom was there, too, and she was afraid. Gerry was hallucinating, grabbing for my mom's necklace. She thought he wanted to strangle her. I calmed her down and stayed next to my brother while they attempted to restrain him enough to put a tube down his throat. I told my mom to leave, to go home. I kissed my brother on the forehead as he drifted off, and prayed to God that he'd be okay. When everyone left, I slumped down . . . and just wept. I cried and cried, until I fell asleep on the floor next to Gerry that night. The nurse covered me with a blanket. Our lives flashed before me like a sad dream. Maybe he wanted a way out.

When I think of children who suffer—
I become sweaty and irritable—
I don't think it's that uncommon
Searching for something else
that could've been—
Then the truth rings clear
That I'm dreaming and so are others—
And we are in a place of holiness—
That God put us here,
And everything is all right—
It's meant to test our strength—

A gift—
And a reminder
To keep dreaming—

I fell deeply into my imagination, subconscious, a dream world. I started to read more, going to the library and devouring anything I could find on psychology, philosophy, poetry. Trying to understand why people were so fucked up. I read Carl Jung, starting with *Memories, Dreams, Reflections.* A pretty heavy read to start down the rabbit hole, but Dr. Jung opened my eyes to the ways of the soul, and my fiery search only intensified from there. I read Robert Bly, Joseph Campbell, Robert A. Johnson, and Marie-Louise von Franz's *Individuation in Fairy Tales.* I felt fairy tales were important, as Grandpa Herman had always instilled in me. I was eleven when he died. My dad struggled to tell me. He knew it was going to be particularly tough on me—my grandpa was my rock, and I felt he was the only one who understood me. I hadn't seen him since we moved, and I was devastated.

I felt so alone in the world. My dad told me his heart failed on the operating table. He also said that Grandpa told him, before he went into the hospital, to not allow me at his funeral, or any funeral—that it was important to him. He knew he was going to die, and he made my dad promise. My grandpa didn't trust doctors. He always said doctors need only a 50 percent grade to pass, it was up to our own selves to stay alive somehow, and it had a lot to do with nature and destiny.

I felt him near me even after his death and wondered if he was still there somehow, a guardian angel. I could picture him and hear him for many years. He comes and goes . . . he hasn't left me.

It's like plugging in
to a light socket
When your true self is
Seen
And the lights go out
when you're not . . .

When I read about interpreting mythology, poetry, art, I felt as if they were clues to living. I was hungry to know how people from all over the world, from across time, experienced love and survived it. My parents were big readers, too, and one day, I found a Shakespeare book in my dad's library. I was stunned—it was so beautiful, like another language entirely. I'd memorize sonnets while on the old exercise bike in the front room watching TV with my dad. I'd learn the first line, then the second, then the third, building them together until I was able to remember it all from the beginning. I felt the exercise bike unlocked the trained mind—a physical distraction to solidify memory. After, I'd recite stanza after stanza to Dad during the commercial breaks of *All in the Family*. He was always impressed. *To be or not to be, that is the question . . .* I still know it word for word. It's one of those things . . . once you learn, you don't forget.

To be or not to be, that is the question:
Whether 'tis nobler in the mind to suffer
The slings and arrows of outrageous fortune,
Or to take arms against a sea of troubles,
And by opposing end them. To die, to sleep—
No more; and by a sleep to say we end
The heart-ache and the thousand natural shocks

That flesh is heir to: 'tis a consummation
Devoutly to be wish'd. To die, to sleep;
To sleep, perchance to dream—ay, there's the rub:
For in that sleep of death what dreams may come
When we have shuffled off this mortal coil,
Must give us pause—there's the respect
That makes calamity of so long life . . .

I never considered college. I didn't even know anyone who had ever gone. I was just happy to finish high school. After I graduated, my dad wanted me to pay rent at home, so I decided to leave. I moved into my first apartment at seventeen and furnished it with a Hudson Bay credit card that came in the mail. I couldn't believe my luck. And I maxed it out quickly. Pink plastic flamingos, tiki bar, margarita maker, round bamboo chairs. It was brilliant. I didn't realize that I had to pay it back—with interest. I was underwater financially right from the start, out of my depth. I had no reference when it came to money.

I also felt it was time to leave home after multiple attempts to rescue my mom from Dad. My mom didn't want to be rescued. I knew I was done the day I saw him trying to hold my mom's face to an element on the stove. From the next room, I heard my mom whispering uncomfortably, trying to make sure we couldn't hear, still covering for him, but I came rushing in and saw them, and something came over me. My blood boiled. I was grown, I was an athlete, I was stronger now. I ran up, out of control, and barreled toward my dad and punched him in the jaw. He dropped to his knees, and I said, with a mustered-up confidence, *Get out of MY house now!* He left the house to go cool off, and when he came back later, we never spoke about it. I was so disappointed in both of them, and in myself for resorting to an uncontrolled violent act after witnessing something violent. Violence begets violence.

It was a turning point, this change in dynamic, and there was no going back. I hated to leave Gerry, but I wasn't far—I was in the same small town—and I knew instinctively that he had to find his own way to cope, even without me. It was very hard on him, to be a young boy trying to protect his mom. He had a lot of anger too, and he hated my father for a long, long time. He wouldn't stand up to him, like I had done. While my acting out shocked my father, I was still a girl, and I think if my brother had stood up to him in that way, there would've been a bigger consequence.

When I decided to leave was when I learned and accepted that I can't change people, I can't save people, only love them. I can only change myself and my circumstances. My mom was never going to leave my dad, and my interfering was only making things worse. This is when I learned the art of leaving. I knew if I didn't get away, I'd be no help to anyone. Freeing yourself is mandatory before you can help to free others. And I always knew when I got on my feet, I'd come back for Gerry . . .

AFTER I LEFT HOME, MY MOM AND I STAYED CLOSE. WE EVEN waitressed together at Smitty's Pancake House. It was a good job and it helped to pay the rent. The tips alone were a lifesaver. It was a busy family restaurant, and my mom was a machine—I couldn't keep up with her. I'd be spilling spaghetti on one person while another man complained that he wanted his eggs *off the toast*. I'd still be apologizing while Mom swung in like Flo from *Alice,* one arm loaded with food, grabbing the toast and dumping the eggs off, saying, *There they are, off the toast!* with a smile and a wink. Then she'd keep on going. The wife leaning into her husband and saying, *See, dear, you could have done that yourself.*

I had a "fan" who came to the diner all the time, a police officer with a massive Chiclet smile. "Sal" was the name on his badge. He knew my car and would pull me over on dark streets to ask me to go for coffee. After hours, he'd sit in front of my apartment in plain clothes in his Jeep "to make sure I was safe." He gave me the creeps.

I was in a pretty bad car accident during this time. I was driving to the ferry to Vancouver to meet some friends who had planned to go see an aerobics competition (so eighties). It was my very first car—my mom had bought it with her waitressing tips as a graduation present. A pale "racing green" MG Midget. The tires were bald, and it had started to pour—plus I could barely see, because my eyes were nearly swollen shut from allergies. I had just rescued two very fluffy Persian cats, and I'd slept with them nestled in my neck—Chico-san Rice Cakes and Orange Julius Caesar. I loved them so much. I'd never had indoor cats before, though, and I didn't realize how allergic I was to them. It made no sense to me—of all people, how could *I* have an animal allergy? I was part animal, I always thought.

I was rubbing my swollen, itchy eyes, trying to navigate the wet and winding roads, when I ended up spinning out. I slid across two lanes of traffic, hit a signpost, and flipped my car off a cliff while turning a sharp corner. When the car flipped, it rolled a full 360 degrees up and over and landed back on

its wheels, on top of a stack of oyster shells. I had been sing-
ing along to "Maniac" from the *Flashdance* soundtrack before I
spun out—and everything happened so fast that the same song
was still playing from the stereo as the car sat there, totaled and
smoking, on a pile of oyster shells. Fanny Bay oysters are fa-
mous all over the world, and every time I see them on a menu,
I think of that accident.

Dazed, I got out and crawled over the prickly shells and up
onto the side of the road. I was wearing white and was covered
in blood from a small head wound that looked worse than it
was. Then I thought of something I'd read about soldiers in war
who lose an arm or a leg but think it's still there. Phantom limb
syndrome. I checked that I had my legs, my arms, my boobs,
my head—then I fainted.

I arrived at the hospital by ambulance. My parents met me
there, along with Officer Sal, who was devastated, practically
in tears, apologizing to my parents. Like it was his fault. I didn't
know this guy—he just seemed to always appear. Dad was so
angry he didn't pay attention to him. He was just yelling and
swearing at me—he didn't have much of a bedside manner.
I later thought it was kind of ironic, coming from a man who
had crashed many cars himself. But this was his way of showing
that he cared. He even took me back to the wreckage after-
ward to show me how bad it was, so I'd understand how lucky I
was to have survived at all. I wondered if his dad had done the
same to him. It felt like some passed-down family ritual.

I loved my dad in all his perfect imperfections. I get it.
Nothing ever made me love him less, nothing ever will.

He is what he was taught. Grandpa Herman was extremely
intelligent, and he meant the world to me. He was so gentle and

wise with me, but when my dad was growing up, my grandfather was a nasty drunk. My dad took the brunt of it, being the oldest boy. That's no excuse, but it left an undeniable mark on him. Later on, I could appreciate the full story.

The best advice my parents gave me
was no advice.
They admitted to knowing nothing
of my world,
my journey
My dreams, passions, and purpose.
They had no way of bailing me out.
They listened,
They worried with me at times,
They loved me the best they could
But it was up to me to find my way through.
When
I understood that,
I was even more free to
create my own life.
It was a blessing.

III

You are not an extension of the small town you grew up in, nor are you your parents or me. You are a brand-new light, given to the planet.
—GRANDPA HERMAN

I NEEDED TO GET OUT OF TOWN AND GET ON MY WAY. WHEN I first made it to Victoria, I stayed with my great-auntie Vie, at my mom's request. My mom was nervous and said she would only feel comfortable about my moving out of town if I was around family to start. Auntie Vie was a character straight out of a movie—feather boas, negligees, wigs, and false eyelashes. She was a widow with a divine spice for life.

Auntie Vie was incredible in the kitchen, her famous pierogies with rhubarb sauce being my favorite. She taught me how to cook—almost everything in tinfoil—and how you must can pickles while wearing a hairnet. *You don't ever want to find a hair in your pickles, dearie!* she'd say. You'd never leave her house without a jar of pickles or homemade mustard in hand. She called herself "the hostess with the mostess" and would spike your coffee with Baileys or Kahlúa liqueur no matter how old you were, with a giggle. She was a love, dreamy yet sharp as a tack. She attributed her quick mind to Nescafé coffee, which she'd read somewhere helped your memory. She remembered everything.

Auntie Vie never had much money, but she lived in a glamorous world she created for herself. She knew what was important. She knew how to live.

Her advice on men was priceless. Auntie Vie said to never trust a man with a wandering eye—*He's most likely a sex addict* . . . She said a woman should have a few men in her life—one for conversation, one for presents, one for sex. It was impossible to make one man responsible for it all. She told me that you get to have only one true love, and once you found it, whether you kept it or lost it, you'd never recover . . . Accepting that was the hardest part. Life was not going to be easy, and you couldn't pretend your way through it. *We're all in the soup together,* she would say. She had already lost the love of her life when my great-uncle died in a tragic logging accident. The rest was filler.

Auntie Vie also shared my love of animals. She fed the homeless "ferals" and all the other cats in the neighborhood, and they ate very well. She'd boil chicken and vegetables, grind them up together, and freeze them in heart-shaped Jell-O molds. She'd wonder aloud why all the cats came to her house, with a wink and a smile. Then one day, late into her eighties, she sadly tripped backward over a cat—a neighbor's Siamese purring at her feet while she was at the refrigerator, waiting for his gourmet treat. She passed away from complications in the hospital after the fall. I can imagine going out in the same way.

I had lived with Auntie Vie for only a few months or so when I realized she had her own sexy life, and I was maybe cramping her style. I came home after work one day, and she met me at the door in a long, flowing white negligee and boa, asking in a whisper if I could come back in a few hours. So I went and sat at McDonald's, drinking water and killing time, trying to come up with my next plan. It was time for me to move on. Auntie Vie and I remained close. I even based my character Val on *VIP* after Auntie Vie—her zest for life and her outfits, her flair for glitz and fun. She was a big influence.

My friend Melanie was living with some girls in a house in Victoria, so I asked her if I could live there with them. There were no bedrooms left, but Mel let me sleep in her closet on a mattress at a very discounted rate. It was what I could afford, and it was all I needed. I was grateful for it. To help earn my keep, I was the one who did the housework, cleaning the toilets, doing dishes. If anyone needed anything, from laundry to errands, they'd leave me a note on the fridge. I slept on the mattress with my pillow surrounded by my shoes. I had about six pairs of high heels in rainbow-bright colors, arcing over my head like a halo in a campy religious painting.

At the time, I had gotten a job as a hostess at the Keg, a local bar/restaurant. I wore the same gold dress every night, an off-the-shoulder prom dress with ruching up one side and ruffles down the other, with matching gold pumps. It was very paso doble. The Keg had a salad buffet on the weekends, and I was allowed to eat from it at the end of the night. I lived off their loaded baked potatoes and would always bring some back to share, along with armfuls of roses from customers. My roommates would just roll their eyes.

Even though I had left Comox, Jack still kept coming in and out of my life. It never really ended—I had to move away. During one of our "off" times, he tried to run me over in his car when he saw me on the sidewalk. Another time, I was walking home and he pulled over and started yelling about my outfit. It was the eighties—the dress was a bit revealing, with big holes cut out of the sides and red waffly stretch material twisted in the front with a gold hoop holding it all together, but barely. It clung to every inch of me—I loved that dress. Jack didn't appreciate my wearing anything sexy, and he told me if I wanted to run around naked, he'd help me, and ripped the dress almost completely off my body. I was locked out of the house—I scrambled to get in, checking all the windows, panicked. Eventually, I just curled up in a ball behind a bush, crying, in almost nothing but my red high heels. When my roommate came home, I was humiliated and still frightened. My friends all knew to get out of the way when they saw him.

Time to move off the island, where he couldn't get to me so easily.

I moved to Vancouver and got a job at Trendsetters, a fitness center. I worked in the tanning salon, and you could really tell. I got free tans, and my skin was so dark, with my big white teeth and pink lip gloss. I was a David LaChapelle picture waiting to be born. Working at the gym afforded me free aerobics classes. There was one instructor who taught a kind of aerobic choreography every week, and had been using my favorite song from *Dirty Dancing*—"(I've Had) The Time of My Life." I couldn't wait to take the class. As I learned the steps and built on them, I would get lost in the song, the crescendo. I got goose bumps when I could dance the entire routine. An accomplishment. Dancing made me feel whole—it set me free.

I WAS SEXUALIZED SO YOUNG THAT I SKIPPED PAST THE PROMIS-
cuity phase. I would only mix sex with love, and as I developed
and grew slowly into womanhood, I had strong fantasies of
true-love stories and fairy tales.

> *My body full of hurt and drama.*
> *Bed alone*
> *Tear-stained pillows*
> *The mirror was an enemy*

During this time, I met a boy, a production assistant and
budding photographer named Mike. He was attractive, suc-
cessful, funny, and worked out at the gym. He needed a sec-
retary to work for him part-time in his studio, and I gladly
agreed. It soon became romantic. I would wear business suits
with garters and stockings under my skirt to the office—I liked
to torture him a bit. He eventually asked me to marry him, and
I said yes. My grandma always told me I should be married no
older than twenty-five, that no one would love me after then,
because I'd be an old maid. *Can't be a quarter century old and not
married!* she'd say.

I always wanted to be a fiancée. To settle into domestic
routines. The idea of a forever someone was exciting, though
something of a guessing game. Mike and I were very sexual, I
guess . . . I didn't have anything normal to compare it to. But
I found a way that worked for me. I loved role-playing. I could
disconnect, be someone who wasn't me. Sex could be fun, fulfill-
ing, and imaginative. Sometimes I would even read him *Pent-
house* letters or do a cute amateur striptease to "You Can Leave
Your Hat On" by Joe Cocker. The movie *9½ Weeks* was my new

obsession. I loved Kim Basinger and Mickey Rourke, and our relationship became bizarrely similar, ice cubes and all . . .

> *I was living in another fantasy—*
> *An omen—*
> *It's just how I did things—*
> *It's how I learned to control my life—*
> *One fantasy after another—*
> *one dissolves,*
> *another appears.*

I thought it was what everyone did. I was able to conquer some shyness this way. It never disappointed. I pushed myself to be brave when everything inside me was crumbling. The engagement did not offer the sense of safety that I had hoped for. Mike became jealous, worried about where I was at all times. He said I was too sexual to be trusted. Later, I found out that he was having an affair with a model who was married—and who desperately wanted to be in *Playboy*. She never made it in, as far as I know. It's funny how things come around.

Living in the "big city" of Vancouver still had its perks. My neighbors were Labatt's beer reps, with a Blue Zone Jeep, Jacuzzi parties, and all the free beer they wanted. One day, they invited me to a Canadian football game—the BC Lions. I didn't really want to go, but my girlfriend did, so we went, decked out in jeans and Labatt's half tops, "Enter the Blue Zone" across our chests. At the game, a cameraman found me and blasted my image on the Jumbotron. My friends made me stand up, and all I could think of when I saw myself up on the big screen was that I didn't like the way I looked. I felt a pit in my stomach. I looked very young for my age, but on that huge screen I thought I looked old and ugly—that was my first, jarring feeling, before I even took in that I was up on the screen in front of the whole crowd. When I did notice, I realized that people were screaming . . . for me?

Someone who worked for the stadium came to get me from the stands to pull me down to the fifty-yard line to do the draw. My friends pushed me to go. I squeezed my way through the crowd and was brought to the tunnel and onto the field. They handed me a microphone and told me to pick a number out of a glass bowl. I spun around slowly, taking in the crowd, who looked like a million eraser heads in the stands, and read the number off the piece of paper, startled by the echo of my voice throughout the stadium. From then on, they called me the "Blue Zone Girl," and the network began using my image in Monday night football ads.

Things went from zero to one hundred after that. Labatt's offered me a commercial and a poster. I said okay but insisted they use my fiancé as the photographer, though he'd never wanted to take pictures of me up to that point. I couldn't really grasp what was happening, it was all moving so fast. I realized then that you could actually make a living this way. I was still giving my parents half of everything I made—I thought everyone did—and I continue to support them now, and will the rest of their lives.

ONE DAY, I CAME HOME TO FIND MICHAEL SUSPICIOUSLY WASHing his penis in the sink. We were arguing because I'd just said how handsome I thought Mario Van Peebles was on TV, when the phone rang. I picked it up with a sigh . . . It was Marilyn Grabowski from *Playboy*. She'd found my number in the phone book. I made sure I said it loud enough so that he could hear— *Playboy?* Michael came flying in from the bathroom, his eyes flashing wildly. He ran into the kitchen and threw a tray of silverware at my head. I ducked behind the counter. Delirious, I listened to Marilyn as she told me they wanted to fly me to LA to do a test for the October '89 cover. They had been looking all over the world for the right girl and they thought it might be me.

Really, are you sure? I asked.

It's up to Mr. Hefner. We'll shoot it and see, she said.

Call me when it's for real, I said, and hung up.

I didn't want to say yes to a "maybe."

Leaving it up to fate.

Almost immediately, the phone rang again. Thank God.

Still dodging forks and knives, I grabbed the receiver— Marilyn said, *We promise it's for real.* I said, *Yes, thank you,* grabbed my purse, and crawled on my hands and knees till it was safe to stand up and run out the door, slamming it behind me. I ran down the sidewalk as fast as I could, him still yelling after me. I couldn't help but giggle at the thought of freedom. And revenge.

I hid at a girlfriend's house for a day or two, and she and I snuck back to the apartment to retrieve a few of my belongings when I knew Michael wasn't home. I told Marilyn I had to leave Vancouver before my fiancé found me. *Playboy* was anxious to get me to LA—this wasn't too long after Dorothy Stratten was killed by her jealous husband, and Hef himself had heard of me already. It was enough to start to worry that our stories were sadly similar.

Back then, you didn't need a passport to go from Canada to the US, just some kind of ID, so I went straight to the airport, so excited. I'd never been on a plane before. At the check-in desk, I told them that I was going to pose for *Playboy*! The woman at the desk said, *Oh no you're not. Do you have a work visa?* What was that? They wouldn't let me pass. I went to a pay phone in tears and called Marilyn. She said, *We'll get you another ticket on another airline.* So I went into a bathroom, changed my clothes—a different T-shirt, tucked my hair into a baseball cap—and went to the check-in desk for a different airline. And, of course, there was the same woman who'd just turned me away, her arms folded, saying, *Nice try.*

Defeated, I called Marilyn again. She apologized and said they would organize the paperwork and asked if I had anywhere safe to stay. I told her I didn't. There was only one other option, a bus across the border to Washington, then a plane down to LA the following morning. So that's what I did. The border officials didn't check me on the bus—they asked the person in front of me and the person behind me. They didn't check everybody, and I got lucky. It was so stressful, but I made it through. *Playboy* arranged a hotel for me near the airport, and I'm sure I imagined it, but I swear there were bullet holes in the door, brown running water, and bloodstains on the carpet. When I finally settled into my room, I threw my hat onto the dresser and took a deep breath. I felt like I was on the run, a fugitive of love, scared and exhilarated. I fell back onto the bed and woke up the next morning in my clothes from the day before. Without changing, I ran out the door. Ready to get on my way.

On my first plane ride, I sat in first class, my eyes never leaving the window. The stewardesses' muffled voices, the smell of food being served—all were lost on me. I was rapt with the view, the clouds, then the lights finally appearing, the traffic, the water's edge, the grid that looked like some kind of brain. A perspective from a height I'd never seen. I fell asleep, perchance to dream . . .

I was jolted awake by the landing, the brakes slamming, my head hitting the seat in front of me—we had arrived. *Hallelujah,* I said out loud, looking around me to strange looks back. I clapped and said, *We made it . . . yayyy!* Maybe a little too loudly.

IV

Playboy was an honor
And a privilege,
I never thought of it as immoral or salacious
but the unforeseen downside
was that it
may have set me up.
It was my choice,
I accepted
my fate.
It gave some
people the impetus, sadly,
to treat me
without respect.
But, I was more used to that.
I wasn't going to be taken down—
I had already survived to this point—
Nothing could hurt me more
Than how I'd already been hurt—
Playboy was empowering—
It helped me in ways I could never articulate—

I took my power back—
I had to—
It was a chance to realize a new life,
A new adventure . . .

WHEN I LANDED IN LA, I WAS READY FOR ANYTHING. I IMAGINED there would be people walking around with parrots on their shoulders, neon palm trees, movie cameras on street corners. The city did not disappoint. I'd arrived on Gay Pride Day, and I couldn't believe my eyes on the car ride from the airport—the intricate floats, the sky-high wigs, the vivid airbrushed makeup, the electric celebratory music, the glitter everywhere. Sensory overload, a dream. Just another day in the life, I thought.

My first day in LA would color me for the rest of my life. *Playboy* had put me up at the Bel Age Hotel in Beverly Hills. I wanted to call my mom right away, but I wasn't sure if I was allowed to use the phone in the room for a long-distance call. I just stared at it. Thankfully, the phone rang, and I picked it up tentatively, like I was on another planet. With an edge of panic, I said, *Hello?*—in the same voice my mom uses when she answers the phone, like you're expecting to get bad news. It was only Marilyn, calling to check on me, and to invite me to "fight night" at the Playboy Mansion. I said, *Sorry, I'm not comfortable fighting anyone,* and asked if I could call my mom. Marilyn assured me that I wasn't expected to mud wrestle. It was just a small, private party to watch Mike Tyson fight on the big screen—and of course I could call my mom, all I had to do was dial nine to get an outside line.

Mommmmmm! I made it! I screamed into the phone. And then I told her, *Not only do gay people exist, they walk around in pink hot pants, handcuffed together, and there is a parade here every day!*

And all she could say was, *Oh, sweetie, it sounds to me . . . like you've arrived!*

ON THE ENTIRE PLANE RIDE, I'D HAD A BOOK CLUTCHED IN MY hand, a worn-out secondhand edition of Shirley MacLaine's *Out on a Limb.* She spoke a lot of the Bodhi Tree bookstore, the place where her metaphysical journey began, and it was on my LA bucket list. So I couldn't believe it when I saw her at the Russian tearoom in the hotel. I was staring at her, probably for too long, just to be sure it was her, and we exchanged suspicious looks. She glanced at me sharply, squinting in a way that I knew meant "fuck off." I looked away, embarrassed.

But I still smiled to myself, taking it as a sign. Synchronicity. I took a breath and ordered anyway. Watching her peripherally was not a crime, and I was starving. The Russian tearoom was the hotel restaurant, where Marilyn had told me I could eat for free—I had never heard of room service. I ordered the borscht, which was a little different from my mom's, as she didn't use beets. And yet borscht is beet soup, the waiter assured me . . . strange. Later, while looking out the window of my hotel room, I was sure I saw Rick James getting out of a car, so I started to sing "Super Freak" while getting dressed. As I was stacking what few clothes I had neatly on the bed, I didn't realize that I was preparing for what would be the rest of my "freaky" life.

That evening, a stretch limo waited at the curb to take me to the Mansion. As I stepped onto the sidewalk, I passed two beautiful men in an embrace, kissing. I said hello and they giggled and pointed. *What?* I said, and then realized they were pointing at my hair—a Sun In spray experiment gone wrong. My hair was the color of a manila envelope. *Honey,* one man said, *that is not one of God's colors,* and he broke into laughter again. I had to laugh with the guys—but geez. I never intended to be blond, I just wanted sun-kissed highlights. Maybe I shouldn't have dumped the entire bottle on my perfectly healthy chestnut locks that sunny day at the beach. *Sorry,* I said, *I know it's bad.*

After a brief drive through the winding roads of Holmby Hills, the limo pulled up to the Rock, the security intercom in front of the Playboy Mansion on Charing Cross Road. The Rock spoke: *Can I help you?* The limo driver said, *I have Miss Pamela Anderson.* They asked for the color, make, and model of the car and then opened the gate. Once inside, a guard asked for the trunk to be opened and inspected it. I asked the driver if people hid in the trunk sometimes, trying to sneak in. *Yes,* he said in a matter-of-fact tone. I had been kidding.

The road curved around through perfectly manicured gardens, finally arriving at a circular drive that ringed a spouting fountain. When we reached the top of the driveway, there was a sign, PLAYMATES AT PLAY. The Mansion itself was like nothing I'd ever seen, a sprawling stone house, more like a castle. Like Disneyland, without the fireworks.

I was dressed in my nicest high-waisted acid-wash jeans and a Metallica T-shirt, little white runners on my feet, ankle socks with the fuzzy balls at the ankles. When I walked in the door, Marilyn greeted me in the foyer and started to make introductions. I wasn't a pop culture fanatic—I rarely knew the names of people or the names of their characters. Was that Tony Curtis? James Caan? There's Rambo, surrounded by pretty girls. I met so many people that night, names and faces I slightly recognized—Chachi, Spicoli, maybe, could that be Cher?—a whirlwind of personalities.

As Marilyn gave me a tour, I was taking it all in—the art, the steamy grotto, the game room. Then she led me to a seat at the bar and left me for a bit. She said she wouldn't be far. I wanted an alcoholic cider, but the bartender didn't know what I was talking about—too Canadian?—so I blushed and ordered a Coca-Cola instead. The bartender had some good jokes, and I was just starting to feel more at ease when . . . oh my God . . . I looked up to see Mr. Hefner as he came down the stairs smiling in his dark blue smoking jacket. Time felt slowed down as people greeted him. He was right in my line of view, maybe on purpose. He looked toward me, and we smiled at each other. I took a deep breath as he passed through his friends and brushed by gorgeous girls politely. But his energy and charm felt directed toward me. I had to look away—it made my skin burn, such a funny feeling. The inevitable shyness. *Well, hello, Pamela, I heard you had an eventful journey,* he said, his pipe teetering in his mouth. I loved the smell of the smoke—it comforted me—and the whole effect was enigmatic. He reminded me of a mythological figure. A Methuselah. With liquid eyes, he looked around at the other men in the room and said softly, *Marilyn is going to take very good care of you. Don't worry, darling, you're safe here.* Then he broke into a character, it seemed, and laughed his famous laugh, and said, *Oh boy, we're going to have to keep an eye on you.* This felt like the epitome of chivalry, a true gentleman—

elegant, passionate, so charming, and yet with that little-boy giggle. It's hard to explain his laugh, but if you heard it once, you'd never forget it.

In an instant,
he became a caricature—
a trap.
I'd relate to that idea later—
being imprisoned by what people expected
or wanted—
Their fantasy of who I should be,
rudely disappointed
if I didn't give it to them.
It affected almost all of my relationships—
not just the romantic ones.
The only ones who saw me
through it all
were the wild ones,
The unsuspecting ones,
The artists.
Thank heaven for them
or I might not
be here at all.

I felt like I had stepped into another dimension—was this even real? How did I get here? It wasn't so far from home, but it was so far out of reach for a girl like me.

I wandered around a bit and was stunned when I saw a Salvador Dalí painting. I asked Marilyn if it was an original. *Of course,* she said. I couldn't believe it. I remarked to her that I loved Dalí, the bizarreness of his perspective, his melted clocks and lens on life, so strange yet beautiful. I even told her how I loved his twirly mustache and how he always wore the same gold lamé vest, going on and on . . . She smiled, a little amused, as did Hef, who was taken aback that I had such a curiosity and knowledge about art and the artist. He already could tell I was different, and he got a kick out of me.

I was getting tired, felt like I'd been hit by a train. As I sat back at the bar, observing the buzz of the room, a man came up to me and turned my barstool to face him. He started rattling off his résumé: *Rain Man, Batman, A Star Is Born.* He seemed puzzled that I didn't know who he was. He continued listing movies off but could tell I was drawing a blank. His name was Jon Peters, he said, offering his hand. *I never come here, but I'm so glad I did. When I saw you, all I could see were teeth and a halo.* Suddenly, Marilyn appeared at my side and stepped between us, gingerly pulling Mr. Peters away. *Nice to meet you,* I said after him.

Marilyn reappeared and explained that he was a very important producer—also having to explain to me what a producer was—and that he wanted to have lunch with me. I wasn't sure why. I remember looking around and noticing how stunning all the women were. Monique St. Pierre, a beauty like I'd never seen, with short cropped blond hair, like Michelle Pfeiffer's in *Scarface.* She wore a long champagne silk gown and held a slim silver cigarette holder, still smoldering, a gentle smoke rising around her. She leaned up against the wall with such confidence and attitude. It was hard not to feel inadequate.

Marilyn felt I'd had enough for the night, and tomorrow was the photo shoot. She told me sweetly that I could come to the *Playboy* photo studio closet anytime, to get dressed for anything I needed to do in the future—lunches, dinners, parties. I was truly grateful but had a hard time imagining what clothes, if any, they'd have in a *Playboy* closet.

The driver pulled around to pick me up. We drove away past a few bungalows on the property, and he told me that was where the Playmates stayed sometimes—*There's the red room, there's the blue room, all with mirrored ceilings.* I imagined as if in a dream . . .

The silk,
the smoke . . .

I almost fell asleep in the car. But not quite. I asked the driver to take the long way back to the hotel so I could see the Sunset Strip. The lights, the Chateau Marmont, the Marlboro man billboard, the Hollywood Sign in the distance. I had never been this tired and excited at the same time. It was like I was floating through space. Into the elevator . . . up to my room, where someone had moved my clothes off the bed. They were stacked neatly on the dresser, and I admired that for a moment, while stripping down to my underwear. I brushed my teeth at the same time I did my leg lifts, touched my toes a few times—a habit I'd gotten into and still a ritual before bed. And finally, I slept.

I DIDN'T ANSWER MY PHONE UNTIL NOON. I WOKE UP STARTLED, forgetting where I was. I was late! The phone was ringing . . . Marilyn—

I'm so sorry, I blurted out, mortified.

It's fine, dear, we're all here and a car is out front when you're ready. You can shower here or do what you need to—no rush.

I got up, jumped in the shower, and ran into the car with wet hair, to find the same driver from the night before, who reassured me we were just three minutes away. We parked right in front of a very tall building with the Playboy bunny logo high up top. Walking in, I was greeted at a desk by a very well-dressed man, who took my name and signature. Behind the desk, there was a large poster of the latest *Playboy* cover, a striking blonde with her finger pressed against her lips. *Shhhhh.*

Inside the studio, the halls were laced with photos of partially nude girls—classy, sheer clothing, playful and beautiful. Some movie-star glamorous, but mostly sweet, shy natural beauties. The girls next door. I could only think of how gorgeous they all were, and what the hell was I doing there?

I was twenty-two when I arrived in LA, with a cute little body. I had never thought I was sexy.

I was only just becoming a woman. I was way behind others my age. I still looked like a baby.

I never felt beautiful
a day in my life.
It wasn't my place
Or my role.
It felt like beautiful girls
Were a different species.
But it didn't matter—
I knew I had stranger gifts than beauty—

This all seemed like a mad plan. I'd fallen down a hole—a porthole to another universe. I was Alice in Wonderland. I walked into the studio, stomach churning. Introductions flew. There was the photographer setting up his camera, some assistants putting lights on the set, a hairdresser, a makeup artist named Tracey with her very new little baby in a sling across her body. They asked me how I'd slept, how I was doing. How was last night? They told me today was just a beauty day, and if I felt up to it later, we could take a few photos. But first, we were going to fix my hair color. Using lots of tinfoil, they gave me highlights—so much attention. Beauty day took all day, and finally my hair was an acceptable shade of honey blond, my toes rubbed and polished a pretty, natural pink. While I held Tracey's baby, we talked about life. I told her I was nervous, told her about how I'd left my fiancé, how he was unkind. I'm sure she relayed all of it to Marilyn and Hef.

I could tell they were digging, and I was offering what they needed. It may have been an unconscious cry for help. They got it loud and clear, and from that point on, *Playboy* was my family.

NEXT, THE SHOOT.

The wardrobe wasn't much—an Oxford blazer, a tie, and a hat. I was talked out of wearing my underwear, which I was hanging on to for dear life, but they promised nothing would show, because I had the hat to cover myself. I was nervous, to say the least.

Okay, let's try one, said the photographer.

This was one of those crucial moments, the ones I soon became addicted to. I had to be brave. Inside my head, I had to overcome what society had convinced me was okay. What I had been taught was a good girl's behavior. I wondered, *How far has that gotten me?* Nowhere. I wanted to break free, break the rules. I'd been programmed to believe I wasn't as good as others. Why did I think it was so bad to be self-aware, or even sexy? What was this fucking shyness? It was paralyzing. A battle raged inside me. I was torn between hurt and confusion while trying to save my own life.

I closed my eyes
as if on the edge of a cliff.
I was about to fall forward into the abyss
and let go of my past,
my bullshit,
everything that had hurt me . . .
Freedom . . .

I opened my eyes
and
FLASH,
first photo.

Then I moved slightly—smiles, no smiles, hat to the side, jacket open. Tracey came back in to touch up my makeup, my lips, my hair, the baby still in her sling. She pulled my jacket open slightly wider. More photos, the photographer saying things like, *Beautiful . . . You're perfect.* Tracey touched my boob to enhance my bony cleavage. They asked me to soften my stomach, saying my ribs were too sharp. I started to feel nauseous, faint, I had to stop. I ran to the bathroom and got sick. My makeup was ruined. I couldn't believe a woman had touched me there, I just couldn't.

Luckily, they got the shot in the first roll of film. I apologized relentlessly, a silly Canadian habit. *Sorry, sorry, sorry.* I assured them I was okay, and we looked at the Polaroids. They put the *Playboy* cover transparency over the photos to show me what the cover would look like. So crazy. It was hard to believe it was me—yet I was still disappointed, somehow. My self-image was so corrupt. It was difficult to accept when I later came to terms with that—I realized I was a work in progress and that my past may have had a serious impact on my self-esteem.

Dinner from Spago arrived—pasta, salad, champagne. I had to have a drink that night—Cristal! Soon to be my favorite. We were celebrating when Marilyn called the set. She said she'd heard the shoot was perfect and that she wanted to take me to lunch the next day at Le Dome. I could come to the studio first, get my hair and makeup done, and get dressed there from the infamous *Playboy* closet.

Le Dome was very chic, the place to be "seen." When I walked in with Marilyn, I was wearing a strapless black plastic dress with black polka-dot stockings and garters peeking out. My hair was up in a chignon, and I wore false eyelashes with a swift, sexy black eyeliner. We sat near the window, on display. She said the artichokes were to die for, that we were going to share one. The artichoke came and Marilyn proceeded to take a leaf off and dip it into melted butter. She put the leaf in her mouth and pulled it out again, moaning with delight. Ha. Was this a joke? A test? I'm not doing that, I thought to myself. I'd never seen an artichoke before, and it seemed like she was having fun with me. I laughed, but then I realized she was serious. This was how you really ate an artichoke. It was delicious.

A man walked up to us—I think it could have been Jimmy Iovine?—and asked if I could sing. I burst out laughing but then told him that I'd played the saxophone in school, and a little accordion with my dad by the campfire. He said, *Oh. We should have lunch. Margaritas! My office is just over there.* Marilyn told him she'd call him to arrange it, and when he left, she said, *Darling, you must know this never happens. Not like this. You're very special. Now, about your plane ticket home. We want you to stay. There is a life for you here.* She said that she was never wrong about these things. Then she pushed further . . .

How do you feel about becoming a Playmate? Hef has seen the cover and has specifically requested that I ask you. This never happens. Girls line up around the block at the Playboy building on Thursdays just to take Polaroids. We choose girls, we shoot them, Hef sees the photos much later and decides who to shoot for centerfolds. And even then, it's not for sure, we may never publish them. But Hef wants you to be a centerfold for February. He's even picked the month. It would mean shooting right away. Oh, and we'd pay you fifteen thousand dollars.

I almost choked on my artichoke leaf. I just stared at Marilyn, searching for the "just kidding." But she looked back at me intently. The only thing I could say was, *I'll have to ask my mom.*

On the phone later . . . *Mom!*

Do it, sweetheart. I'd do it if I were asked. Don't look back, stay there, don't come home—live a new life—

I could hear the tears she was trying to hide.

Maybe one day we can come visit?

She was letting me go into the world. And I know she wanted me to have a different life than hers.

This is your chance, baby girl.

V

A FEW DAYS AFTER MY LUNCH WITH MARILYN, I FINALLY MET WITH the relentless pursuant Jon Peters, the producer I'd been introduced to at Hef's party. I told him over lunch at the cafeteria at the Columbia Pictures building that *Playboy* wanted me to be a centerfold, and Jon protested:

I'll pay you double not to do it.

I'll take you shopping.

You can live in one of my houses in Bel Air.

Let me save you a lifetime of pain.

I told him nobody was going to make that decision for me. But he still insisted. I refused his offers, at first. But he talked me into moving to Bel Air. Then the gifts started pouring in and I couldn't help but accept—it started to feel rude not to. The doorbell would ring, and a chauffeur would bring me a little red box from Cartier, Ralph Lauren, Azzedine Alaïa. I was measured and had things tailored, bespoke—a backless tux, like in *Flashdance* (Jon produced that film), hats, gloves. I couldn't resist—it was fun! Surreal, à la *Pretty Woman*, and so chic. I wore riding pants, boots, and crisp white shirts, though I had never ridden a horse. I carried a Tiffany Filofax and wore a Cartier Tank watch. He'd call me over, patting his lap for me to come sit, and then present a diamond tennis bracelet. It was becoming more and more like that. Then he said I could use his cream-colored Bentley, with his driver at my disposal, and of course have my own Mercedes 420SL convertible when I wanted to drive myself. Which was never.

My next-door neighbor was Ronald Reagan. I had maids (who practiced opera singing in the garage), a cook, and a hip rabbi to teach me Kabbalah. I thought Kabbalah was beautiful—I wore the signature red string on my wrist. I love ritual and religion, even if I've never joined one tribe.

Jon lived in a separate exquisite home, not far away in Beverly Park. He'd been in Los Angeles for quite some time, starting out as a hairdresser. Now a major movie mogul and studio head to be reckoned with, Jon would pop by unannounced, and we'd go for drives in his Range Rover, or on his Harley to the movies, or to Montecito, where he had put in an offer on San Ysidro Ranch. It was listed for around ten million dollars at the time. I could not comprehend that kind of money being talked about so casually. He acted like he was talking about ten dollars, and I would just think . . . just add zeros.

One afternoon, I arrived at Jon's house to play tennis wearing cutoffs, so he drove me to a store in the Valley for sophisticated tennis clothes—the short white skirt, et cetera. On the way back, the car's horn got stuck. It was like we were in a parade, blaring through Beverly Hills. Jon just about lost it. He made a dramatic call from the hardwired phone in his car, alerting someone on his staff to meet us, that we were on the way. Not that they couldn't hear us coming. When we approached the house, he was so overwhelmed, he jumped out without putting the car in park and it almost drove through the garage door. Luckily, one of the guys raced over and hopped into the driver's seat, to my rescue. I thought it was funny, but Jon was fuming. He got over it fast, though, and soon turned it into entertaining storytelling for our lunch guests.

We didn't even play tennis that day, but I wore the outfit while we had lunch with his friends. Jon was a consummate showman, and depending on the audience, his stories would change, different variations right before my eyes, to different people. He's in the right business, I thought. I eventually realized Jon actually believed the crazy stories he told. He lived in his imagination, like me—it intrigued me, yet his tendency to embellish was a known phenomenon. Jon had a lasting influence on me, though. His powerful creativity, his boldness, his style, and his confidence.

Mario Van Peebles called me from the set of *21 Jump Street* in Vancouver. I'd always had a mad crush on him, having met him once when I was an extra on the show—since they shot the show locally in Canada, a few friends were extras, and they'd brought me along the day they were filming. It was fun, but I'd had no desire to be an actor, and definitely not a model. It felt empty, shallow, and weird. It just wasn't me.

Mario had heard through a mutual friend that I was now in LA, and was just calling to say hi. We talked a little, and I was so embarrassed, my cheeks were burning—I didn't know what to say. He told me he'd like to take me to dinner when he came home to LA the following week. I squeaked out, *Sure*. He was amused by my shyness and asked where I was staying. I gave him the address in Bel Air, and he laughed and said, *Oh-kayyyyy* . . . probably thinking it was strange, since Bel Air is for the extremely wealthy.

Several days later, the front gate bell rang. When I opened up the door, I had on my riding gear, black boots, khaki pants. A white billowy blouse and a blue velvet riding jacket with tails, a wide-brimmed hat, freckles, and a shy smile. I looked straight out of a Ralph Lauren ad, wholesome and healthy. Mario was so handsome. He asked me what I was doing there, and I said, *I live here.* He asked, *Why? With whom?* And probably wondered, *Where is her horse?* I told him that someone had given me the house. He had more questions, but finally I said, *This happens to everyone!* He said, *No, this does not happen to anyone.*

We went to a nice dinner, and then we went dancing. He spiraled me around in restaurants and nightclubs, running from one to the next—it didn't matter where, or if anyone else was dancing. We ended up tangoing through the streets all night long. It was a perfect evening.

When he brought me back to my house, we kissed, and he said patiently, but with sincere concern, *I think you need to get your things and get out of here. Take only what you brought. There's more to this story, and I'm afraid you won't be able to get out of this if you wait too long.* I was shocked at this—it just sounded ridiculous. But Mario insisted that soon there might be no way out for me. He couldn't believe Jon had never come on to me, but it was true. He was flirtatious, friendly and funny, but I didn't get that kind of pressure from him. He'd asked for head rubs and for me to tickle his neck, but no more than that.

The more I thought about it, the more I started to realize that maybe I had been conveniently blind. I couldn't deny that.

I was ashamed of it, and when I had lunch with Jon the next day, I told him I was uncomfortable with our relationship. That I didn't want to give him the wrong impression. He brushed it off—ever the great deflector—and said not to worry, then asked me whether I'd like to plan a dinner party for him. It was a clever distraction, and I perked up, excited by the idea of it. I was living a dream.

Jon called me "Bump Bump," he said, because I was always so determined. And this task was no exception. I planned what I felt was a very elegant affair. A plethora of pink garden roses, petals spilling all over the table, and homemade place cards with swirling calligraphy. A fizzy pink champagne upon arrival. And as for the menu, I had the chef carve as much of the meal as possible into heart shapes.

I wore a long white silk Ralph Lauren dress and hardly any makeup, except mascara and lip balm. Jon had cut my hair so it framed my face, with the perfect fringe, and he stood behind me while I faced the mirror and put my hair up with one long French curved pin in a chignon. *Like Brigitte Bardot,* he said. Then he surprised me and attached two little diamond studs from Cartier to my ears. I felt like a princess.

The guests were Hollywood heavy hitters—producers, directors, studio heads, and their glamorous wives. Everyone was so complimentary—*How sweet!*—but it also felt slightly condescending, and I soon realized it was a little much . . . I had gotten carried away with the hearts.

Jon put me on a pedestal—I was on display. During the dinner, I was the star of the show. He bragged about me endlessly, made me feel special and talented. It was part of his charm. He allowed me to shine like I never had, and I think it may have been a little refreshing to the group that my efforts were pure, unpretentious, and different from the usual.

Jon persevered. Following the dinner, he offered to fly my mom out to visit. It was her first time on a big plane. Before that, she'd only been on a tiny seaplane, and it had crashed into the ocean on takeoff. They all had to be rescued. She was pregnant with me at the time. I always thought maybe I wasn't meant to be born. But I fought to be here.

To arrive to such grandeur must have been overwhelming— the drivers, the attention, the California landscape with its palm trees, soft sandy beaches, and roaring waves. Even the danger- ous swells felt magnetic. From all our conversations, she felt like she'd already been there, and I had prepared her the best I could for the attention she was about to receive. We had more dinner parties at Jon's house, with a spilling overabundance of hydrangeas and fragrant garden roses, each room exquisitely styled with Tiffany lamps, layers of contrasting textures, woolly Navajo fabrics, ornate Turkish rugs, Remington bronze, and Baccarat crystal sculptures. Jon had the best of everything. The guests were suspiciously friendly. Mom almost fell over when strangers kissed her on the cheek, thinking that only happened in movies.

I brought my mom to the Mansion to meet Hef. She thought he was out of this world—though it did start off a bit awkwardly. Hef made a bad joke to her about how I couldn't af- ford clothes when I got there, and they both laughed nervously. I felt a twinge of discomfort but brushed it off, thinking we were all just slightly new to each other. My mom was taking it all in, getting attention from others, when Hef leaned in and asked me if I'd consider cohosting a new *Playboy After Dark* with him. He'd sent me tapes of the old version, but I hadn't watched them. And I also knew Jon really didn't want me to pursue more associations with *Playboy*.

Hef wanted to talk to me about being Playmate of the Year. He told me, because of the Gulf War, the *Playboy* higher-ups felt they had to pick an American girl. So it couldn't be me. I appreciated that he wanted to break the news to me directly, but I didn't even know there was such an honor or how that could even become political. All of us Playmates were engaged in the fight. Doing all we could to boost morale. I remember Operation Playmate fondly. We wrote to soldiers, and letters poured back in. Some notes to me were accompanied by photos of my image etched into the side of a tank or plastered on the wing of a fighter jet. I think that was way cooler than being Playmate of the Year.

On the way home, Mom was locked in a stare out the window, commenting on the night and how Hef was such a gentleman. *A lost art!* she said. She also wondered aloud if Elvis had ever been to the Playboy Mansion. She always wondered about Elvis.

Mom thought Jon was terrific, too. It's hard not to be seduced by so much when you come from so little. Jon kept telling her we were in love, but I didn't think of him that way. It was becoming awkward. I knew I couldn't do it any longer. Before my mom went home, she looked at me knowingly and just said, *Follow your heart.*

So I did. After Mom left town, I found an apartment, bought an old BMW that needed bungee cords to hold the doors closed for $500. It smelled like dead people, even with the pine tree air freshener hanging from the mirror. I left the key to the Mercedes on the table, packed my backpack, and left. On the run, again.

The apartment I found was about an hour east of LA, in Newhall. A recommendation from a friend. It was harder than I thought to rent a place on my own, being an out-of-towner, out-of-country. It was good enough for me. I took in my surroundings. I had one fork, one spoon, one knife, a plate and a glass (a handy starter package I'd picked up at the gas station). No furniture, not even a bed—just some blankets and a few books. I sat in the middle of an empty room and contemplated my life. How did I get here? I had nothing left but my self-respect, and that was enough.

I remember sitting in that empty apartment with its freshly painted powdery white walls, reading *Nightwood* by Djuna Barnes and Doris Lessing's *The Golden Notebook.* This was a time of seeking the depth in things, and coming to terms with my own wants and needs.

Dr. Margie Paul was someone I met through Jon. She had written a great book on inner-child work and had given it to me. She thought it would be of interest after getting to know me at one of our dinner parties. She was right. Studying it brought tremendous insight, and I responded well to taking inventory of my life through that lens. And once I opened that door, I met people who would change my life forever. A healer named Charisse, who helped me get in touch with my own gifts. And Dr. Silvers, a Jungian analyst whose teacher in Switzerland had been part of Carl Jung's inner circle. Dr. Silvers and I talked about all sorts of illuminating concepts. The shadow, alchemy, and the unconscious. The documentary he shared with me, *Matter of Heart,* piqued my interest in dreams and the anima and animus, and we would often talk about them in hours-long sessions.

My conversations with Dr. Silvers were expensive but lifesaving—a worthy investment. I felt like he recognized me, understood me. Like my grandfather had. Dr. Silvers would prescribe challenging poetry, from Dylan Thomas to Goethe, as well as helpful books like Alice Miller's *The Drama of the Gifted Child* or Joseph Campbell's *The Hero with a Thousand Faces.* He encouraged me to draw mandalas that peeked into my psyche. Our meetings stimulated me—I started to realize how my dreams, my imagination, and real life were all of equal importance.

As much as I was pouring into myself,
I felt I was pouring out.
I had been working on myself my whole life
But there were times I abandoned myself, too:
A consistent dichotomy.

I went on a few more incredible dates with Mario during this time. I loved his house, so sculptural, refined and wild at the same time. He had a Tarzan swing in the bedroom. Ingeniously, the shower watered the garden. Mario's mom lived with him at the time. She was one of the first environmentalists I ever met. They used no perfumes or chemicals, and organic everything—so progressive and inspiring. His father, Melvin, was a director and rumored Black Panther. I found his stories intense and fascinating.

I was a seeker, soaking up as much information as possible, engaging in lively discussions. I'd read Angela Davis and James

Baldwin, and admired their work. I wanted to know more about the Weathermen and their antiwar sentiment, about Harvey Milk's quest for LGBT rights. I was searching for a feeling I couldn't find—life was a complete mystery to me, ruled only by faith, destiny, and the universe. But knowledge and exposure to new and radical perspectives helped me find my way. As crooked as the path was, I was learning and growing, thorns and all.

Mario was proud of me for leaving Jon's world. It was not easy for a girl like me, in my circumstance, living off the little money I had from my *Playboy* appearance, to have enough self-worth to leave someone who was willing to take care of me while the future was a question mark. I had no fallback position, there was no going back. I was willing to take the risk and bet on myself. It was common knowledge that these rich and powerful men ate new girls up, promised them the world and spat them out when it was time to move on to the next starlet. I'm glad it never came to that.

Mario and I hiked to the Hollywood Sign. We made love for the first time in a field of long, soft grasses, as horses ran by dangerously close, almost trampling us. Mario lifted me up and wrapped his arms around me. He closed his eyes and told me to close mine. *Pamela,* he said. *I'd like to propose* . . . My eyes shot open, and I punched him in the arm. I started laughing uncontrollably, telling him not to ever do that again. *I almost thought you were proposing!* His eyes were still closed, and he said, . . . *that you have lunch tomorrow with me and my mom.* It was a strange, suspended moment, and later it hit me that he might've actually been proposing. The way a proposal should be. Unsolicited and unexpected.

THE MOST DIFFICULT WORK FOR *PLAYBOY* WAS SHOOTING THE centerfold. It was true, what other Playmates said, *If it doesn't hurt, it doesn't work.* They shot it with a Hasselblad, a large-format camera, using single eight-by-ten sheets of film. Each shot was very deliberate. You had to move slowly, be put in position and hold it, looking relaxed and sensual without breathing. I learned about body parts in a whole new way. "The return of the breast" meant that part under your arm, where your breast meets your side/back. And it was important to point your toes . . .

The photos that accompanied the centerfold were taken with a thirty-five millimeter—"small camera"—which allowed more freedom to move around. They'd scheduled my shoot at a lush, rambling estate in Pasadena, amongst fountains and intricate secret gardens and mazes. Very Versailles. It was to be soft and sensual, natural. And in my favorite element, water. A gateway. Where I was comfortable. Connected to my truest self.

This is where
A creature was born.
I started to play
With a depth of character—
Someone living inside me
That wanted out.
And yet who I could detach from,
partially,
Keep at bay.
Someone
I could call on . . .
And be at any time.

I did what I thought all models would do, but a heightened version. I was wild and uninhibited, rolling, laughing, playing to the camera, pulling the cold, wet silk across my skin . . . goose bumps, biting my lip. I had unleashed a wild woman inside me, but the shyness crept in. I was the girl next door, pushing boundaries, naturally coming into her sexual existence. For *Playboy*, that's exactly what they wanted.

It was authentic
All happening on camera
In real time.
Hef called me
the DNA of Playboy.

The Mansion had an annual Midsummer Night's Dream party. All the women wore lingerie and the men bathrobes. "Everyone who was anyone" would be there. I was getting to know more of the girls. They usually introduced themselves with their first name and *Playboy* centerfold month: *Hi, I'm Martha, Miss July 1973*. All ages, from the start of the magazine. I was always happy to see the gorgeous ladies of the sixties, seventies, eighties—so many beauties. Even Bettie Page was there. Everyone looked refreshingly different—different hair colors, bodies, tones of voice, lipstick colors, interests, dreams. Each unique to herself. Many of us would end up in the grotto, splashing around nude. It was a primitive reverie—free and uninhibited and wonderful. *No clothes*, Hef would say, *lint gets in the filters!*

You had to be screened and accepted to get into the parties. A ratio of two or three girls per man. It was always a good time, and quite innocent for debauchery. Sexy, classic, playful, wildly entertaining, and just plain old-fashioned fun. How often can you say all those things together and still feel good about it? That was *Playboy,* somehow it just worked. It was a beautiful and sensual chaos. Only Hef could pull this off like a gentleman and get away with it.

Still, there were some inevitable disappointments. A few flies in the ointment. I remember being at an appearance in another city with a few other Playmates. When one of the male guests asked me to get in a Jacuzzi with him and offered me $10,000, I said, *That sounds like more than just a Jacuzzi, no thanks.* Field trips always got a little weird. The girls got mad at me after I told Hef—I became known as a "tattletale," but for a good reason. I was worried about their safety. Unfortunately, some felt the need to make a little money on the side. It was not typical, though, and Hef would have been through the roof if he knew the extent of it. There were explicit rules in place. *Playboy* did everything they could to protect us. Though some slipped through the cracks. One of the girls asked me to go with her and a few others to an island somewhere. A thousand dollars a day, just to hang out by the pool. Again, I said, *No, sorry.* It didn't sound like just "hanging out." I'm pretty sure I saw in the press later that a group of girls, some ex-Playmates, had been held against their will in another country and barely made it back alive. I felt like Mr. Magoo, guided to safety by angels at every near wrong turn.

At the Mansion's parties, people were tangled together in every nook, seminude, sprawled on silk cushions or rolling in the grass. An actor I recognized, Scott Baio, came and sat down next to me on one of the pillows. He slid my high heel off to check my toes, then pulled my hair back to see my ears. Looking for defects? I giggled and let him chase me all night. We ended up dating for a while, but his family was very protective of him (and his money), and I'm not sure they wanted him dating a Playmate. And they were furious when he let me drive his Mercedes convertible.

You never knew what you were going to walk into. A labyrinth of cleverly designed powder rooms meant for discreet naughtiness, each with its own full-length mirror, chaise longue, sitting area, and private bathroom. I don't want to give the wrong impression—*Playboy* was no orgy. It was rare to walk into someone in the act, but people might bring girlfriends for a little extra fun. And this is where I came upon that actor from *One Flew over the Cuckoo's Nest*. Mr. Nicholson had two beautiful women with him. They were all giggling and kissing up against the wall, sliding all over each other. I walked by to use the mirror, bending over the sink to fix my lip gloss. Trying not to look, but I couldn't help myself and caught his eye in the reflection. I guess that got him to the finish line, because he made a funny noise, smiled, and said, *Thanks, dear.* He's told that story a few times, so I don't feel bad repeating it. I saw him years later at a dinner party, and he asked me with a mischievous smile if I remembered how we met. Really? How could I forget?

VI

I was in another world
One I understood less and less
No blueprint
I told myself I had to stop worrying.
I just had to go for it:
Knowing I would fall into traps
And make mistakes.
You can think your way out of living.
This is when I learned
To flip the script—
When you change your thoughts,
you change your life.

CASTING DIRECTORS FOR TV AND FILM WERE CALLING THE *PLAY-boy* office, looking for me, after my first cover came out. There was a lot of unexpected interest. Something called *Baywatch* was calling relentlessly, but their offices were in Marina del Rey, and that sounded far away. I'm not a natural driver—I'm easily distracted—so I turned it down. I was still shooting covers for *Playboy,* traveling, signing autographs. But I agreed to do a cameo in *Married . . . with Children.* It was a pillow-fight scene, which seemed easy enough.

I had just finished rehearsing my scenes with Al Bundy and was on my way to the car when a woman stopped me and said, *You're late for hammer time.* I was confused. Was she talking about an MC Hammer video? *They're still seeing girls! You have to come.* Intrigued, I followed her. We stepped into a room with a line of cute girls holding scripts, sitting in chairs lined up against a wall. The woman dragged me past everyone and pushed me into a room. I turned and there were about a dozen people staring at me. The camera light came on, and they said, *Count backward from ten and say your name.* I don't know what I did that was so special—maybe the look of confusion, a deer in headlights—but I got the job. It was for Lisa the Tool Time Girl.

Home Improvement became a big hit. *Here you go, Tim,* was my only line every episode, and when they decided to expand my part, it was, *Here you go, Tim. Have a nice day.* It was the most popular show in North America. On the first day of filming, I walked out of my dressing room, and Tim was in the hallway in his robe. He opened his robe and flashed me quickly—completely naked underneath. He said it was only fair, because he had seen me naked. *Now we're even.* I laughed uncomfortably. It was the first of many bizarre encounters where people felt they knew me enough to make absolute fools out of themselves.

The first time I was ever recognized was at an ATM. I was wondering how the car full of boys knew me as "Lisa," until I realized I hadn't changed out of my overalls and work boots, my tool belt still hanging on my waist. After that, it became a constant—no time to process my feelings about it, no frame of reference. My life was changing quickly, and it was something I accepted and learned to deal with over time.

> *I imagined a*
> *Kabuki-esque drama.*
> *My life*
> *A pastiche.*
> *Sitting in a theater with popcorn,*
> *Watching.*

Baywatch kept calling. My boyfriend, David Charvet, was auditioning, and I agreed to accompany him. David was drop-dead handsome—they were lucky to have him there, and he really wanted to be an actor. The casting director ate him up, then looked past him to me and asked if I was actually *the* Pamela Anderson. The one who never showed up. I timidly said yes, I was. The producers came out and offered me a job right then and there. David got the part, too, though I don't think he was too happy that they hired me as well. David knew this would be the end of us, somehow. I tried to tell him it wouldn't change things, but he was right. We didn't last long.

The producers wanted to know more about me to create a character. We spoke about my grandfather and how I loved the ocean, animals, crystals, how I could feel energy. That's how C. J., or Casey Jean, came about. The bohemian free spirit who loved incense and candles, a healer and an animal whisperer. A true reflection of me.

It was getting hard to juggle both *Home Improvement* and *Baywatch,* so I had to make a choice. *Baywatch* seemed to be more fun—I loved being outside, swimming and spending time on the beach, learning about the ocean. And I loved the physicality of doing my own stunts, diving, driving Jet Skis and the Scarab. So much better than being on a soundstage. I brought my dog, Star, to work with me every day, and the cast and I became very close. I ended up making my career choice based on quality of life—*Baywatch* paid less, but it wasn't about that. The scripts were easy, and my silly photographic memory came in handy. There was much more to being an actress, I learned later, but in the meantime . . . I was excited, grateful to be there, and loved every minute of it. Yet, I was treading carefully, slightly unfulfilled—something stirred.

The *Baywatch* years were a blur. By the fourth season, I was the highest-paid actress on the show. Many of the international broadcasters would buy only the episodes I appeared in, so there were "Pamela clauses" in the international deals. *Baywatch* was shown in 150 countries. At the time, I didn't even *know* there were 150 countries. Billions of people watched it, and soon, it was the number one show in the world. The C. J. *Baywatch* Barbie was a bestselling Mattel toy, though I didn't financially benefit from that. I had menial representation at the time, and nobody foresaw the success. It all happened so fast.

My very first film was a classic. I played a concubine who also happened to have a secret twin. *Snapdragon* co-starred Steven Bauer—Steven had been in *Scarface* and in my favorite coming-of-age film, *Thief of Hearts*. Looking back, I think I did a pretty good job in that film. I had read *Acting: The First Six Lessons* by Boleslavsky before we started filming, and I tried to apply it to my work. It involved dredging up memories and embodying characters with parts of actual people from my own life. It was thought-provoking and therapeutic—I really had no idea what

I was doing, but fantasy was something I'd honed my whole life. I was learning, experimenting. The Method approach appealed to me, tapping into observation and empathy. Even as a secret-twin concubine. We all have to start somewhere . . .

Playboy wanted to shoot me in Cuba, adding that President Fidel Castro wanted to meet me. I had been curious to visit the island but Steven advised against it. He told me about his family's struggles there, living under a dictatorship. I wasn't sure what that meant entirely, but it frightened me. I told *Playboy* I had to reconsider.

I had a semi-naïve fascination with revolutionary politics. A Che Guevara poster hung on my wall, I read *The Prison Letters of Fidel Castro,* and I loved *The Motorcycle Diaries* so much, I'd even bought a 1970 Norton motorcycle as a birthday gift for a boyfriend. I moved all the furniture out of my living room and placed it by the fireplace. We made love on it by the roaring fire.

He was into the Beat Generation—Bukowski, Ginsberg, and Henry Miller, whom I also loved but found a bit crude. I was more drawn to artists like Anaïs Nin and Frida Kahlo. Their sensitivity. Frida's sad and painful self-exploration affected me deeply—I read her memoirs and her poetry and have gathered all her writings over the years, learning all I can about her. I was so moved by her artwork, the reflection of her difficult romance. You could sense in her art how she loved and protected Diego Rivera. How she allowed him to be himself at great cost to her own happiness.

I also felt a kinship with Anaïs Nin. A soul connection. I wish I could have met her. We spoke the same language—one of eroticism and tension, of despair. And, as with Frida, I craved a person in my own life who might recognize me as an artist, someone who understood that I was a far cry from what people thought of me.

> *I needed someone to see me*
> *Through the fog.*
> *How could they?*
> *I was guilty of painting my own self-image.*
> *But nobody knew how far I'd come—*
> *Layered in transparencies*
> *Projections magnified*

How could I expect anyone to love me enough to see through it all? They had nothing to go on but this image being flung into the world. No matter how I tried, the image was bigger than me and always won. My life took off without me. It felt superficial, materialistic. I joked that my breasts had a career of their own, and I was just tagging along. Flashing back to the gym at the Playboy Mansion, where I agreed to amplify my chest like everyone else, then endured years of sordid attention I wasn't ready for. Then came complications, the unexpected injuries that led to more surgery, a vicious cycle. I was fine the way I was. Someone once told me, when it came to surgery, it's a paradox. *You may gain something, but you always lose something when you mess with Mother Nature.* I understand that sometimes it might be worth it, or necessary. In my case, it really wasn't. It was an impetuous, shallow decision. Un-thought-through. A part of my charm.

> *I ached*
> *For a purpose*
> *I had so much to give . . .*

I felt like
I had accomplished nothing.
But I was determined to do my best.
My life was still a gift
and I wasn't one to complain.
I just wanted to figure out the best way
to handle things.
To use my influence
For good.
Pure intentions
No matter what the world thought . . .

This was when I decided to turn my kind of activism into something full-force. I wanted to share the international attention I was getting with something more meaningful. Animal welfare was a continued priority, so I wrote to PETA to ask if I could be of any help. They were happy to hear from me. My first campaign was "Give Fur the Cold Shoulder." A billboard in Times Square. We had already started our letter-writing campaign to world leaders and other influential people. I learned much about world politics, diplomacy, and persuasive correspondence. PETA and I have been connected ever since, with great, worldwide success.

FAME ISN'T SOMETHING YOU CAN PURSUE, AND IT'S CERTAINLY not something you can stop, even if you want to. It just happens—and with it, the craziest moments. Ridiculous, impossible things you can't imagine. I know I couldn't have imagined them.

Like when I found out that John F. Kennedy Jr. wanted to meet me. He wanted me to pose for the first cover of *George* magazine. I wasn't available, but he didn't give up. Eventually it happened—a shot of me stark naked, hiding behind an American flag. He rang me at the shoot, apologizing for not being there. And I thought, Thank God he isn't, I'd be too nervous. I was embarrassingly giddy on the call, making noises I didn't recognize—some kind of squeal? I couldn't get off the phone fast enough. He was so charming, I was blushing, and I'm sure he could tell over the phone. I was out of my depth, in maybe my most embarrassing moment. He tried again to reach me after the shoot, but I was too shy to call him back. He was way out of my league.

It was becoming increasingly difficult to shoot on location, because fans from all over the world were flocking to Will Rogers beach, where we shot *Baywatch*. They'd come see the filming, but many of the fans were concentrated around Tower 14, C. J.'s lifeguard tower. We found ways to film, despite the throngs of people. The show must go on.

Contractually we were obligated to promote the show, and I was being chosen more and more for the international appearances. While on a PR tour through South America, we stopped in Buenos Aires.

Inspired by the atmosphere and my love of dancing, I decided to see some tango at the Rojo Tango show at the Faena Hotel, which was the best venue for it in the world. It was electric. Hearing the familiar box accordion of my childhood played in such an exciting, powerful, and provocative way. Watching the dancers, sensual, slow, and purposeful. After the show, we went backstage to meet them, and I asked one man if he could teach me to tango. He was probably eighty years old, almost blind. We arranged to meet in the ballroom of the hotel the next day.

Tango is about a relationship. There are only four steps—a deliberate game of cat and mouse. As we started to dance, he put one hand on my lower back as his other hand greeted mine ever so gently. He would barely touch me, but I'd know to move with the smallest gesture, to come forward or step back. We effortlessly fell into a rhythm together as I let myself go. Even the heel flicks came naturally. If I went the wrong way, he'd stop me gently and say, *Just allow me to lead you.* It brought tears to my eyes to just trust in this way.

It was one of the most sensual experiences I've ever had. I was left strangely breathless, wanting more . . . A true man leading a woman. Something I'd never felt. I was so connected to this man I barely knew. I was connected to the experience . . . It changed me, and I've never forgotten it.

Wading in cool water
Gardenias
fragrant
and other flowers,
Preciously
surround me . . .
I spin
Nude among them
They stick to my oiled body
White on tan skin
Goose bumps.

Long gone
The feelings
of innocence
of wonder
But music remains
I will find you
at the end of a song

We also traveled to Chile, where I insisted on going to Pablo Neruda's home at Isla Negra. He was my favorite poet, and even though I didn't speak Spanish, I would read his poetry out loud in his native tongue. It felt important to feel his original rhythm, his cadence. Even before I read the translations, I somehow already knew what he was talking about. At Isla Negra, I met a friend of his who had cared for him in his later years. She knit me a shawl and told me stories of a painful history. Pinochet. Innocent people sunk to the bottom of the ocean. I visited the prison, Villa Grimaldi, and it was heart-wrenching . . . the artifacts, the proof of treachery. There remains speculation that Neruda might not have died of cancer but, rather, had been murdered at the hands of Pinochet's regime.

I made it a habit to go to museums, historical sites, and galleries, and to talk to local people everywhere I traveled. My thirst for knowledge. I was an empty vessel, and I was filling and filling me. Insatiable.

I needed my own security team. Their presence became essential—a fact made clear during my visit to Punta del Este, a wealthy resort town in Uruguay, when I was almost trampled to death. During a scheduled appearance, I began to walk through a crowd to get to a stage when the crowd started to swell. I kept feeling hands touching me, grabbing at me—more and more of them. Six police officers flanked me for protection, but I was being squished on all sides. Rocks and sticks started being thrown—it was turning into mayhem. A rock hit me in the head as the crowd yelled, *We love you, Pamela!* I was starting to get scared. My personal bodyguard, Brian, put me over his shoulder and pushed through to get me into a van. The windows were broken, and the crowds were rocking the van and almost rolled us. As far as you could see, there were teenage boys. Thousands of them. They tore down the stage I was meant to stand on. My clothes were torn, too. We were lucky to get out of there. Cameras recorded the incident, and it made international news. My mom was watching CNN and thought, That poor girl. Then she realized it was me . . .

Though my center was calm,
A meditation
I always came back to—
I am safe
I am protected.
"The world is a safe place"
was my mantra.

Celebrity felt like
A strange disease
You couldn't wash off.

VII

Little did I know
I was about to be swept right off my feet.
The beginning of the end—
and all the greatness in between.
True love was only a heartbeat away—

AS A WOMAN OF SELF-DISCOVERY, CURIOUS ABOUT WHAT LIFE could bring me, I thought I'd ring in the New Year the only way I knew how—with a clean slate. A new business, something unexpected. I was ready for anything. What you put out into the universe has a way of finding its way back. And for me, it's like a boomerang.

It was that New Year's Eve, at a bar I co-owned with some friends, called Sanctuary, that I met Tommy. I sent a shot of Goldschläger to everyone in the VIP room; I think Tommy thought I sent it to only him. He came bounding over to my table, wallet chain swinging, no shirt on, just tattoos and nipple rings. He sat beside me and licked the side of my face. In turn, I licked the face of my best friend, Melanie, and she licked someone else's face sitting next to her, and so on. Mel is still my best friend (surprisingly). She'd taken a leave of absence from work in Canada to come down and assist me on the movie *Barb Wire*. She had no idea what she was in for.

Tommy and I had been staring deeply into each other's eyes for a few minutes too long when Mel pinched me and said, *Nooooo* . . . She pulled me out of the seat and said, *Let's gooooo* . . .

Tommy followed us to the car; he wanted my number. Mel said again, *Nooooo.*

As we were peeling out, I leaned my body out the window and called out to him, *I'm staying at the Chateau!* We watched each other with an undeniable interest till we were out of each other's sight. I've never felt such a force of nature or pull of gravity. Melanie would have none of it! She said, *I can tell he's not good for you. I'm worried* . . . She is a sweetheart, but we are very different, like all good friends should be. Yin and yang.

The next morning, the phone in my hotel room kept ringing over and over. Finally, I picked it up, and it was Tommy. I said hi . . . I looked at Mel mischievously, and she was giving me that "you better not" stare. Out of nowhere, I channeled a voice, not my own, deep and sexual . . . and purred, *I want twenty-four hours with you, then I never want to see you again,* and hung up. I looked at Mel and smiled, and said, *There, I'm sure he won't call back.* Mel just put her hands up to her face in shock, laughing.

When the phone rang again, I pressed the speaker button, and Tommy was singing, *My bologna has a first name, it's L-A-R-G-E* . . . I laughed and hung up. He called back again, and Mel picked up, saying, *Pamela isn't here. She's in the spa getting her nails done.* Tommy called the "spa"—there was no spa at the hotel. Mel and I left the hotel that afternoon, while Tommy went shopping at the Pleasure Chest, an awesome sex shop on Santa Monica Boulevard, hoping for those twenty-four hours with me. I listened to my friend reluctantly and let it go, leaving it to fate. I had a funny feeling, though, that he'd find me somewhere, somehow, some way.

When I left the hotel, there was no easy way for him to track me down. A few months later, he finally did. He was determined, it was impressive. My Malibu condo on Point Dume was under construction, so I was staying in a temporary apartment in Marina del Rey. I had a voicemail service at the time that would screen my calls. If someone called two times quickly in a row, I knew it was my agent, and I would pick up. I had a photo shoot in Mexico the next day and was about to walk out the door to go to the airport when the phone rang once and then rang again. I was sure it was my agent—but it was Tommy.

Hi, beautiful. He sounded a little sad.

Hi, I'm sorry but I have to leave. I'm on my way to Cancún . . . in Mexico, I said (as if he didn't know where Cancún was, but I had just learned).

Without me??? he said mischievously.

No, no, no, please don't go to Mexico. You wouldn't . . .

I'm coming, I'll find you. Where are you staying?

Please, Tommy, no . . . I'm going for work! I hung up and ran out the door to my driver, thinking he wouldn't dare.

I still don't know how he got my number, but I checked my voicemail from Mexico and it was full of messages from Tommy. *I'm on my way!* and *I'm on the plane eating peanuts and drinking whiskey!* I let my girlfriend and makeup artist, Alexis, listen. She was quite intrigued—Alexis was a lot of fun, and loved men, to say the least—but I looked at her and said, *No.*

Tommy had left his hotel phone number and room number on my voicemail, but he didn't know where I was staying. All the same, I told my hotel's security, *If you see anyone with tattoos, please don't let him in.* I thought he'd never find me, but Cancún is small. At dinner on the final day of shooting, a little bored, I said to Alexis, *It's our last night here. Let's call him. Let's have a fun night. We leave tomorrow . . . What could possibly go wrong?*

I ended up extending my trip . . .

At the time, I was in love with Kelly Slater. We were dating, but he was still on and off with his ex-girlfriend, and I was starting to get that feeling of wanting to get married and have babies. Kelly was a world-champion surfer by then, the best in the world. He traveled a lot, but we were growing closer. He was a true free spirit, bohemian, gentle, wise, with such beautiful eyes, like a cat's. I didn't mean to hurt him, and he was my first phone call after the wedding.

Tommy and I were officially married by the time we left Cancún. The club we ended up in that first night together was called La Boom. Tommy must have slipped something special in my champagne—the room got warm and fuzzy, and my skin felt like butter, even softer than usual. He said, *Let's get married,* and I dreamily said, *Okay.* He took the skull ring off his friend Bobby's hand and put it on my ring finger.

The next morning, Tommy called everywhere to find an available minister—*like, now.* The minister met us on the beach, and a few friends we'd met the previous night were our wedding party. I was in a bikini, Tommy in board shorts. We sat on lawn chairs sipping chi chis with the pastor. After the ceremony, we all jumped in the ocean together, wanting the ocean's blessing.

On the flight home, I asked him what our last name was, and he said, *Lee.* I said, *Oh, I thought it was Tommy Lee . . . something. Jones?* Then I asked him where he lived. He said, *Malibu Road.* How perfect—it just kept getting better. We were in heaven, never letting each other go. And we spent a lot of the flight in the "mile-high club" bathroom; we were even applauded when we came out.

We landed to a sea of paparazzi. It was shocking. We'd been stupid enough to use disposable cameras during our night out at La Boom, at the wedding ceremony, and during who knows what else, then developed them at a one-hour photo place near the hotel. We weren't exactly in our right minds, to say the least. I guess the shop made copies, because they were all over the tabloids by the time we arrived back in LA.

My second call, after Kelly, was my mom. News crews had already surrounded her house. She was furious. *Who's Tommy?* She couldn't believe I had gotten married, cried that she had always dreamed of being at her only daughter's wedding. With every call after that, everyone was more and more angry. Gerry was more shocked than anything. He was living in LA by then. When he'd finished school, he'd gone to work on a commercial fishing boat in Alaska, but I convinced him to come to LA. It was to be us against the world. He was working as an extra on *Baywatch* and performing gigs in a grunge rock band he had put together. He was just starting to get his own life together in LA and was not too happy to learn he had a new brother-in-law. We had always been so close, and this was something he'd thought he'd be a part of. My decision to marry without my family present was definitely out of character. But I was genuinely happy. Lost in a sea of love.

When I moved into Tommy's place on Malibu Road, we each weren't even sure what the other liked for breakfast. Do we drink coffee or tea? We knew nothing of one another outside our ecstasy-induced love weekend in Mexico, but it all felt completely genuine. We had no doubt in our minds we were meant to be.

An adventure:
Love at first sight started to melt
Into day-to-day life—
We were stronger together.
It felt natural.
So impossibly in love—

In those first few weeks, we barely left the bedroom. We took calls from friends in bed, like it was our office. It felt very John Lennon and Yoko Ono (*give peace a chance*). Tommy played guitar naked and made up songs about us. He would look at me with so much love and would sing about anything, even my toes. He loved my feet.

Tommy was the man of my dreams—so handsome, tall, fun, covered in a thoughtful story of tattoos. His patchouli fragrance comforted me. I was mesmerized, entranced by his low, sexy voice. We burned nag champa incense, listened to music, and made love all day long. Being with him, I felt complete.

Tommy started looking for our forever house, where we could start a family. We bought a big, beautiful home in the Malibu hills—Spanish Mediterranean, with a touch of Japanese bonsai. Tommy is an amazing gardener, artful with plants and koi ponds. Together, we tried to create an oasis. Our remodeling was endless, and with it came the typical marital squabbles. Tommy was one to spend days debating cost, colors, finishes, styles of doorknobs; I liked to dream it, get some fabric, and start stapling it to the walls, see my ideas, an art project in evolution. One morning, I woke up before Tommy and re-upholstered the entire powder room in yellow fake fur—with a zebra toilet seat. I rehung the iron mirror and some vintage *Kama Sutra* drawings. It was fabulous, and a big surprise for my husband when he woke up. We had fun, and our rule was no rules, even with our idiosyncrasies.

But it was hard to live a normal life—the paparazzi were everywhere, hanging from trees, pointing cameras at our house. I remember lying in bed reading and Tommy walking by, wallet chain swinging, over to our sun deck, a sawed-off shotgun in hand. He pointed the gun at the camera crews and yelled, *Get the fuck out of here!* For a "wedding present," *American Journal* didn't press charges.

Our lovemaking was always tender, delicious—never dark or weird or trying too hard. We were connected. Sex was fun. Our bodies were in sync, and we craved being close, never far out of reach or out of sight of one another. I went with Tommy to the studio or he came with me to the set. But it was a challenge. We couldn't move around easily—we were always photographed, chased, provoked. We tried to get used to it, but we were wearing down, fast.

Our spirits were what held us together—
And I was willing to do anything
To make it work

I always wanted to be somebody's angel—
I was full of surprises
Especially for the man I loved.

It was uncharacteristic of me to be mysterious or keep secrets, so Tommy became increasingly agitated when I suddenly wouldn't answer his questions about where I was or who I was on the phone with. He may have even thought I was having an affair—never have I, never would I—but, in reality, I was secretly planning "Tommyland," the birthday party nobody will ever forget.

I dreamed up the party from a bubble bath, scribbling ideas on a yellow legal pad. Stacks of legal pads were always handy—it was where most of my ideas were born—and this bathtub had some magic in it. I decided we would take over a ranch not far from our house, turning the place into an amusement park–meets–fever dream.

A surprise.

About twenty-five friends were invited, musicians mostly. I had asked everyone to dress in crazy costumes, drag-anything. I was the ringmaster, decked out in a Mad Hatter top hat, thigh-high boots, and fishnets, while Tommy donned a custom royal robe and a magnificent crown I'd had set with precious stones and vintage jewels.

On the night of the party, Tommy had no idea what was going on. I'd convinced him to allow my makeup artist Alan to do his white clown makeup. He initially protested, bratty, questioning everything, whiskey in hand, till I placed the robe over his shoulders and the crown on his head. Then he realized what he was going to be getting into. His tone changed when a tour bus pulled up, the guests piled into it, music blaring, champagne flowing. We arrived at the ranch to a red carpet being rolled out by little people, through the gates of Tommyland. The whole entrance was a scene: tiki torches, glitter and pink rose petals being thrown, people on stilts and Cirque du Soleil performers covered in chalky makeup, their muscular bodies highlighted, it seemed, by the moon, but really by a strategically placed blue light. They moved in slow motion to the music, balancing off of each other, a show of impossible strength.

The event was a feast for the eyes. At every turn there was another surprise: a singing Elvis duo with swinging rubber penises, Polynesian fire dancers, circus mirrors in the bathrooms. There were more performers than guests. I commissioned a huge swing ride, a Ferris wheel with lipstick cameras mounted strategically, and a *Stomp* wall of percussion instruments—lots of things to make noise with. Tommy's friends were mostly drummers, and they went crazy on it. An ice-cream bike was driven by a scary clown through the crowd, ringing his little bell, while cute girlfriends we knew sauntered around the party with appetizers dangling off their buxom bikinis—stuffed grape leaves and spanakopita triangles in honor of Tommy's Greek heritage. Meanwhile, our friend Blue circled the room with Scooby snacks in his turban. Another guy was literally the birthday cake—he was dressed as Mighty Mouse (Tommy's first tattoo) and you could eat his shoulder pads, a cake on each shoulder. I'll never forget the look on Tommy's face when he saw that cake—he curled his lip and looked at me sideways, like it was the best night of his life. He had a big knife in hand with that crazy smile. Perhaps a little dangerous for Mighty Mouse. He was already pretty wasted by the time he cut pieces for everyone.

In addition to the party, my gift to Tommy was a grand piano, custom-painted with designs swirled in gold leaf, inspired by his tattoos and Polynesian drawings, reminiscent of Bora Bora—a place we both loved and eventually traveled to together. Posted next to the piano was a tall, Dr. Seuss–style twisted candelabra, its wax dripping down its wrought iron and onto the stage.

It was magical, cinematic, like a short film made without the intention of ever being watched; a memory lived, captured, without ending. Some of us poked our fingers with pins and signed the guest book in blood. A sacred bond, a ritual.

Just as the sun was peeking through, the sky a gorgeous fire orange, a Starbucks truck pulled up, as did ambulances I'd hired to take everyone home. Our guests left on stretchers as "patients" got mouth-to-mouth from . . . whoever, sirens singing softly, lights pulsating gently off into the sunrise. Down a long, winding road. Epic.

Our lives were a living, breathing Fellini film. Most of my friends, the ones who really knew me, told me I should be a director, a photographer, a songwriter—anything creative. I just wasn't sure how to manage anything like that while I worked every day. But I was known to throw the best parties in the universe.

I spent all I had on that party. It was worth it. And money wasn't something I was comfortable hoarding. If I had it, I only wanted to use it to make people happy.

Love is the quality of attention we pay to things.

VIII

AFTER A VERY SUCCESSFUL AND WILD TRIP TO THE CANNES FILM festival, the movie *Barb Wire* was green-lighted. Nobody knew how well received the idea would be. We started shooting right away. The schedule was taxing. It was my first introduction to such long, long hours, involving exciting and dangerous stunts that I did mostly myself. Learning to ride a motorcycle. Kickboxing in a tiny, restrictive corset. Rolling around while shooting guns like Desert Eagles and assembling at hyper speed MP5K fully automatics.

My new husband was with me on set every minute. He'd wait for me naked in my trailer, and when I came back to rest between scenes, he'd purposely mess up my hair and makeup and unlace my corset. A tactic used to spend more time together. Because I was his, he'd said. He wanted his "wife time." All of his antics kept getting us in trouble. One day, Tommy punched the producer in the face after he'd been told to go home. And was banned. But he would have none of that. He would park his car next door—his black Ferrari Testarossa was easy to spot—and he'd just jump the fence to be with me in my trailer. I was used to his behavior and initially thought it was funny. I interpreted it as his showing me how much he loved me and that he needed me to show him more attention.

It was a challenging time. I hardly slept, I was working constantly between the movie and *Baywatch,* and I was freshly married. It felt like I needed to be "on" 24/7, and yet I could barely stay awake. Then a girlfriend introduced me to something that would keep me going a bit longer. I had never been into harsh drugs—these were speedy diet pills, ephedrine she got from her boyfriend. I liked how the pills kept me awake, and I could get a lot more done. But the side effects meant I was losing weight fast. I looked like a bowlegged skeleton in a bathing suit, 105 pounds at five foot seven. In some of the *Baywatch* episodes filmed during that time, even the tiniest waves would knock me over. Everyone began to get concerned, and rightly so. I started to withdraw, keep to myself on and off the set. I was worried about upsetting Tommy. He got so angry and jealous when I had scenes with other men, especially if I was kissing someone else. That was out of the question. They started changing the dialogue and scenes if they saw Tommy coming. I even wore a pager on the back of my bathing suit on set—"007" meant "call Tommy now." *Baywatch* was like my family, and they could see how this stress, pressure, and desire to make everyone happy were affecting me.

One day, I didn't show up to set. It wasn't like me, I was never late to work. I was always early, in fact. The driver, Fal, came to my condo to find me unconscious on the floor. He picked me up, put me in his truck, and drove straight to the hospital.

I had been at the end of my rope. I was confused, sad, tired, not in my right mind. I had gotten into the bathtub the night before and tried to swallow a bottle of Advil with vodka, sinking slowly under the water. But luckily, I couldn't stand the taste of hard alcohol and the nausea forced me out of the tub. I threw up everything, all over the stone floor, and then fell asleep in a pool of Advil-red vomit. It must have looked scary.

The day before, Tommy had rammed his car into the makeup trailer, punched the cabinets out in the makeup room, and thrown me into his car, driving off the set, tires spinning. He dropped me off at the condo and went who knows where. I cried all night. I couldn't take it anymore, and I didn't know what to do. It was a depth of despair I'd never felt—and I'd been through a lot. I loved Tommy, and I hated more than anything to upset him.

Gerry was working as an extra on *Baywatch*. When he got to the set in the morning and heard about what happened, and saw how shaken everyone was, he got ahold of Tommy, and they both met me in the hospital. Tommy was apologetic, in tears, afraid he'd almost lost me. Still, he and my brother started fighting, rolling around, wrestling, throwing punches. The staff tried to stop them, and next thing, security was trying to escort both of them out. When the doctor came in, my brother was furious and screaming at Tommy, saying he was killing me, and most definitely killing any chance I had at a career. The doctor tried to speak but couldn't get a word in. When everyone calmed down, he firmly presented a fact. Tommy straightened up. The doctor said I was pregnant. We were totally blindsided, a happy surprise. All was forgiven, and we fell into each other's arms in happy tears.

I was on bed rest, but sadly, after only a few weeks, I lost the baby. I had a miscarriage. We were devastated. I blamed the pills, the lack of sleep, the workload . . . everything. After that, we both became super healthy. We slowed down the best we could. Tommy showered me with attention and sweet surprises. Things seemed to be getting better.

I was still filming *Barb Wire* and, as soon as I was feeling better, had to get back to work. But as I was doing a back roundhouse kick in my stilettos and corset, an ovarian cyst burst. I screamed and fell out of frame to the floor. Everyone ran to me, and Tommy pushed them aside and scooped me up. He ran with me cradled in his arms to his car and drove to the hospital, the movie's insurance van speeding after us. I was okay, but Tommy would not leave my side.

I had to stay in the hospital overnight. Tommy and I made love in the narrow, stretcher-like hospital bed while I was connected to an IV. We fell asleep in each other's arms. There was no way they were going to be able to get him to leave—they didn't even try.

A FEW MONTHS LATER, WE DISCOVERED I WAS PREGNANT AGAIN. We were over the moon and felt so blessed with baby Brandon in my tummy. We treasured every pregnant moment, taking nothing for granted. We carried the ultrasound photo with us everywhere, I hired a midwife, and Tommy was in the gym lifting weights with his trainer every day. We were closer than ever and couldn't wait to meet our baby boy. I loved being pregnant, and we both enjoyed witnessing the changes in my body. I wore a bikini by our pool at nine months "pregos." I continued to work, but only gently, until I was about six months pregnant, when it was too much to hide beneath the red swimsuit.

Brandon was born at home, in our bedroom. The midwife arrived with everything we needed for the birth. I wanted a natural birth and didn't even take a Tylenol—there was no way I wanted any drug in my body that could harm my son. I wanted to give him the best chance possible. We put on a sooth-ing soundtrack—Enigma—and when he was born, "Return to Innocence" was playing. It was twenty-one hours of labor, in the bathtub most of the time, though technically Brandon was born next to the tub—it was too complicated to move back in once we got closer to the birth. Tommy must have smoked about ten packs of cigarettes on the deck of our bedroom while I was in labor, pacing back and forth, telling me I was sexy when I was screaming. That's really not something you want to hear at that time, but we were laughing through the tears. My mom was there, and she held my hand throughout. Star, our golden retriever, stayed snug to the door outside the room.

We gave birth
to a gorgeous, blue-eyed baby boy—
Brandon Thomas Lee.

Swaddled and perfect
His little face scrunched up,
already curious,
and looking at us like we were crazy.
We called him
Our baby burrito—

Tommy and I were mesmerized by our son. Tommy would cry holding him, singing to him. I loved to film Brandon every day. We met every milestone with cheers and tears. We were all together every minute, all so in love.

WE DIDN'T LEAVE THE HOUSE FOR A LONG TIME AFTER BRANDON was born. It felt risky, since our home was surrounded by paparazzi. We took some quick family photos with a photographer we knew and trusted, just to release something to the press, hoping that might just get rid of the constant paparazzi and even civilian curiosity. The unrelenting surveillance. But it was short-lived—the photographers, and some fans, were absolutely merciless. The paparazzi still came after us, running us off the road at times to get a picture. We had to take most of our appointments in our home, even the pediatrician, Heidi Fleiss's dad, Dr. Fleiss.

On our first date night out, Tommy and I went to the Viper Room, leaving Brandon with my parents. My mom encouraged us to go. I think she saw how we needed our alone time, and she felt that Tommy needed to know that things could still be fun, even with the added responsibilities. But when we left the club, a photographer jumped in my face with a big, bright blinding light. *Where is your kid?* he yelled. *You drug addict!* We were shocked. I said, *He's with my mom, and I'm not a drug addict.* Tommy stepped in like a madman, ready to kill. He shoved him hard, while another photographer farther away filmed us. It was a setup. They knew we most likely had a few drinks in us and that it was going to be easy to get a rise out of Tommy. They were right. Tommy sent him rolling down the hill, breaking the guy's hip. Then another photographer pepper-sprayed Tommy, and some got in my face, too. Not as much, but it was still hard to breathe.

I yelled, *Fuck you, fuck you, fuck you,* pointing to all the cameras. Everything was filmed. We peeled out, but soon our driver had to pull over because Tommy was in so much pain. We looked for a garden hose in someone's yard to wash his eyes out. All the while, still being followed and filmed, like the paparazzi were parasites we couldn't shake. It was all over the news.

The paparazzi made our lives extremely difficult—they would antagonize us, especially Tommy. Any man would want to protect his wife and family. The lawsuits kept stacking up. We were leaving a hotel, and Tommy dropped his cigarettes. I bent down to pick them up, and a photographer whistled. Tommy walked up and had a few words, then backhanded him, breaking his jaw. Another $25,000 to settle that one. There were court-appointed anger management and therapy as part of that, too—with a therapist named "Dr. Weiner." We loved Dr. Weiner, his name especially. He tried, to no avail, to teach us to think of the paparazzi as invisible. He explained that any reaction from us was what they wanted, and if we looked past them and ignored them, the photos wouldn't be worth anything. It was a test of will, he said.

Easier said than done.

We needed to move to the moon, we thought, to get away.

It felt like we couldn't go anywhere, and it was taking its toll. There were car chases, sending people off the road into ditches, rocks through windows. Tommy and my dad formed ranks and became vigilante defenders with their own style of street justice. Mulholland martial law. My father was rocking a very seventies style at the time, with a strange goatee. He wore Hawaiian shirts and mirrored sunglasses, like Hunter S. Thompson. It was quite the look.

He and Tommy would go running after the paparazzi together. Tommy would go one way and my dad the other to get them from both sides, making sure they couldn't get away. Dad even jumped a fence at full speed to chase a photographer, eventually grabbing his camera and holding it under a fountain. Another $25,000. My dad never understood why we couldn't protect ourselves without being sued. He joked that for fifty bucks back home, we could make these idiots go away for good. *It's LA, Dad,* I said. *Different rules.*

Before we knew it, Tommy and I happily became pregnant again. Despite the chaos of everything around us, this was the most blessed time of my life. Pregnancy suited me. I had more energy than ever, and I was lucky that Tommy loved my pregnant body.

I was determined to give birth underwater this time—I was going to stay in that tub, no matter what. The labor was less than half the time of Brandon's—only nine hours—and I had the energy to see that through. We put on Enigma, and again, "Return to Innocence" came on right when our baby arrived. I will never forget seeing Dylan floating under the water, still attached to me, looking straight into my eyes. It was one of the most amazing experiences of my life.

He was so peaceful
An angel—
My little Buddha baby—
It was as if he looked down
And chose us—
He knew we needed him.
Some serenity . . .

Butterflies would land on Dylan—
His energy is still that Zen—
My beautiful butterfly boy.

I FINALLY SAID GOODBYE TO *BAYWATCH* **TO FOCUS ON OUR FAM-** ily full-time. I was content, and nothing else could hold my attention. I couldn't imagine being away from my beautiful family. By then, I had already moved my parents to Malibu. They were living in the condo I'd kept on Point Dume. I didn't trust anyone to help with our children other than family. We had no nannies—Tommy and I were going to raise our own kids. God help them.

IX

We never made a "sex tape."
We just filmed each other, always,
and lived a sexy passionate life:
sweet newlyweds.
Just
two crazy, naked people
in love.

A SAFE THE SIZE OF A REFRIGERATOR WAS STOLEN OUT OF OUR house. Inside had been our important papers, jewelry, keepsakes. Tommy's collection of guns. At the time, Tommy was rehearsing and recording with Mötley Crüe in our garage, and we had construction going on in the main house.

Tommy decided to get something from the safe, which was well-hidden behind a carpeted wall in the garage. But when he pulled back the carpet, it was gone. The entire safe! He came running upstairs, asking, *Where's the safe?* We thought it was a joke at first.

It didn't take long to realize that it had been stolen and could have been taken anytime during a three-to-six-month span. We hadn't checked on the safe for a while, not since we had installed and hidden it. It was so huge, it had to be an inside job. We were completely shocked. We tried to remember what was stored in it. I knew the bikini I was married in was in there, a collection of champagne corks with special occasions written on them in Sharpie, the scroll on which Tommy had written the poem he read to me at one of our weddings. The one where he'd ridden in on a horse, my knight in shining armor. We had a lot of weddings.

Then, strangely, we got a message from Bob Guccione of *Penthouse*. He warned that he had a video of us having sex. He offered five million cash for the rights to them. We were in shock, wondering if it could even be true—we had no memory of filming anything so crazy. We told him to go fuck himself. And that we wanted back any tapes he had in his possession.

Not too long after the crazy Guccione offer, Tommy caught something on the news.

Fuck—whoa, he said.

What? I asked.

He told me to go upstairs—he didn't want me to see it. When he came up a few minutes later, he told me there was a tape for sale, and a porn actress was impersonating me out in front of Tower Records, signing copies.

Later,
a VHS tape came to us
wrapped in brown paper.

Too late.

I didn't watch it,
I have not watched it to this day.

But Tommy did. He told me they'd spliced together a lot of different things and made it look like we were filming ourselves having sex all the time. He said it was nothing too bad—but bad enough to be hurtful to me, and he was so sorry.

I looked at Tommy with utter disbelief, barely comprehending what he was saying.

I felt strange,
liquid,
melting . . .
Leaving my body once again

Then I looked at
my growing belly—
I had to be strong
Realizing
For the first time
That this was not one of those times
I could disappear.
I had to stay present.
I had to stay in my body
I had to feel this
and find a way through it.

Once we got our head around what was happening, we attempted to block the cheesy company that distributed it, with the help of the attorney Ed Masry, who had approached us once the news went wide. He was as disgusted as we were and felt it was an important case regarding privacy rights.

Tommy and I weren't allowed in the deposition room together; they had to interview us separately. They chose to depose me first, trying to hurt us the most. I was seven months pregnant with Dylan at the time. I was feeling strong when I walked into the room, but my heart sank when I saw there were naked photos of me blown up and placed behind the lawyers seated across the table. Such a cruel tactic, apparently done to prove I didn't care about being nude publicly. One lawyer was literally foaming at the mouth, white stuff collected in the corners. You could smell his sick and unrelentingly nervous breath from across the room.

They explained that I had no right to privacy because I'd appeared in *Playboy*. Then came question after invasive question—about my body, sexual positions, sexual preferences, locations I had sex in—and suggestions that I probably liked the attention. I thought, What does any of this have to do with them stealing or selling our private property? Ed told me I didn't have to answer their questions, but it all seemed so ridiculous, it was hard to keep my mouth shut. I held a protective hand over my pregnant belly, willing myself to stay calm.

I endured days of harassment from the lawyers and from this scumbag, the tape's evil distributor, sitting at the end of the table, pathetic and small. Meanwhile, Tommy paced outside in the hall, biting his nails. Eventually we had to move him into a separate room, to make sure he didn't pass the idiots in the hall or run into them in the bathroom. God forbid.

I did my best to stay calm, but the long hours and the horrible things they were saying took their toll. I was stressed, hurt, humiliated, sad—in shock that these grown men thought so little of me. They didn't even know me, I thought. Why do they hate me so much? I had a hard time sleeping—I had a new baby at home and one on the way. We just wanted to find some peace and enjoy our new family together.

Afterward, Tommy held me, kissing my forehead, and said, *They can't do this to you, baby. They can't do this to us. I won't let them. It's over. We need to let this go. We have each other, we have our kids to think of—and that's it. Fuck them all.*

Tommy and I instinctively knew that the health and welfare of our baby was the most important thing to consider now. Ed understood when we told him to drop everything, that we couldn't deal with all this stress, especially me. I was so worried about how it would affect Dylan—we knew he was feeling everything I was feeling, and that wasn't fair to him.

The damage was done.
Our response—
Fuck them.
Hold our heads high
Let it go
And move on with
Grace and Dignity—

We called it "G and D" for short, something we said to each other every time things felt out of control. Tommy was a rock star, and even though this situation hurt his heart, this was only going to add a little color to his legendary career. Not that I was overly ambitious for a career as a serious actress, but we both knew, inevitably, any chance of that was over.

Despite the hurt, the pain, we did what we said we would—focused on our family. We went internal, burrowed in. The first page of the photo album/scrapbook I made us was emblazoned with the title *Everyone Sucks but Us*. Tommy would kiss my big pregnant belly, with Brandon in between us, as we promised each other that we would get through everything. And that we'd try with all our hearts to just move on with our lives. Dylan was born that December, a healthy, beautiful, wonderful boy.

They ended up making hundreds of millions of dollars off the spliced-together home movies of us. We endured years of embarrassment, harassment, and stress—not to mention what our families went through, our parents, our siblings, and how it affected our kids when they got older and were teased in school. *Playboy* was innocent . . . this was much harder on everyone. It was one of the most difficult things I've ever gone through. It is still a great cause of pain for all of us.

It ruined lives, starting with our relationship—and it's unforgivable that people, still to this day, think they can profit from such a terrible experience, let alone a crime.

Sinking into despair, at times
it reminded me how I disliked
humans.

Dirty money,
Unforgivable.
Karma.

NO MATTER HOW STRONG WE THOUGHT WE WERE, IT TOOK ITS toll. Tommy and I were overwhelmed. We were chased by paparazzi while rude comments flew, even when we were holding our boys. Brandon learned early how to give the middle finger to photographers. I didn't approve, but Tommy thought it was funny.

We were so tired, overwhelmed. One night, both babies were settling down, and Tommy was on the floor, rocking himself back and forth, holding his head and mumbling, *What about me? I want my wife back.* I was cranky, sleep-deprived, holding Dylan while Brandon was in his playpen, reaching out for me and crying, wanting to be picked up.

I told Tommy that I'd call my parents to come help, just so we could talk or be together. I went to the phone, but he grabbed it from me, saying, *NO! I don't want them here!* I snapped at him, *Then fucking help me! You have to grow up, Tommy. It's not just about you anymore.* I'd never spoken to him like that before, and he lost it. It was a Tommy I'd never seen, didn't recognize. His eyes went black as he grabbed the phone away from me, twisting my arm as I was holding Dylan in the other. My nail tore off, blood dripping down my arm. The kids were so frightened. I picked up Brandon, too, but he slid frantically down my leg and held on to it tight, hyperventilating. Tommy ripped Brandon off me and threw me and Dylan into the wall. I was so scared he was hurt—he was screaming and he was only seven weeks old. Tommy ran out the door with Brandon, who was reaching for me—*Mommyyyy!* Tommy took off running down the street with him. I could barely breathe, trying to catch my breath through the tears. Panicked, I called 911. The police arrived at the same time as my parents.

I was bleeding and marked up, in shock. The police pressed charges—they had to, with or without me, when they saw my condition. When they asked if there was a gun in the house, I naïvely told them yes, there was a Glock handgun in our bedpost. Tommy was on probation and was immediately arrested. He went to jail. Our hell began.

The divorce from Tommy was the hardest, lowest, most difficult point of my life. He wrote to me every day from jail, but I wouldn't talk to him or visit him. I was crushed. I still couldn't believe that the person I loved the most was capable of what had happened that night. We were both devastated, but I had to protect my babies.

We vibrated together
unrequited, fated—
but impossible, forbidden, lost.

Years later, I sadly discovered through a friend that Tommy may have been taking steroids for a short period during that time, and that may have been part of the reason he snapped. But then, we all search for any excuse for the people we love.

The rest of my life, my relationships paled in comparison. It was a losing battle. It wasn't the others' fault—they just had no shot. My relationship with Tommy may have been the only time I was ever truly in love. I know a lot of that may have to do with his being Brandon and Dylan's father. Inherently, children are the memory of the love it took to make them. And every time I looked at them, I saw Tommy. Nothing I did could stop the pain. There was no replacement. I felt like a failure. I blamed myself and I blamed Tommy for the fact that we could not keep the most important relationship of our lives together for the boys. We let them down.

X

To love anything is to accept its loss
—UNKNOWN

I expected marriage to be forever
God knows
I've proven that theory wrong
time and again.

I never believed in trying to change people—
Just change husbands.
We are all on our own path.
We are new worlds to one another—
And really
Life's biggest challenge is to be enough for one's self.

I FELT LIKE A LOST SOUL, DRIFTING AIMLESSLY. I HAD TO BE
strong for my boys. And I'd find every way to do that. I learned
the importance of self-care. Breathing correctly, a healthy diet,

and forcing myself to exercise. Meditation and prayer were life-saving. And reading was an elemental way to process my feelings. Joseph Campbell's *The Power of Myth* sat at my bedside, while Kahlil Gibran's poetry and stories seemed a comfort, and fitting.

I wanted to learn all I could about male psychology, to try to understand the patterns of behavior that had tortured me and to make sure I raised healthy boys. I dove into *Iron John* by Robert Bly . . . and there it was: "The key is under your mother's pillow." That struck me. A mother-son relationship is a complex one. I had to raise my boys with all my heart, but I also knew that one day the boys would have to leave me to grow into healthy, self-sufficient men.

When I read Robert A. Johnson's *He, She,* and *We,* my world was turned upside down. Johnson talks about the myth of romantic love and how an intense, fairy-tale love is unsustainable over a length of time. Tristan and Isolde, Romeo and Juliet—tales with echoes of tragedy. I assimilated this and began to recognize the impulse in myself.

It was the worst. I couldn't reconcile the love I had for Tommy, as a man, as a father, and what I was supposed to do for the greater good.

Once he was released from jail, we'd have secret meetings, breaking the restraining order. He'd tap on my window, and we'd make love in the car outside my house. I was under the strict orders of lawyers and therapists to avoid him, but we couldn't help ourselves. We ended up right back in each other's arms. It didn't last long, though—neither of us could forgive the other, deep down. We just weren't equipped to get through it all. I loved to see him with his boys, but the four of us together forever was only a dream.

I LOVED OUR COTTAGE, A REFUGE RIGHT ON THE BEACH. WE lived in The Colony, the only gated community in Malibu. Our shingled home was cozy, all roses and French antiques. I tried to create a place of safety and stability for my boys. Nothing felt better than living at the water's edge.

My parents were coming to town, so I asked the housekeeper to prepare the guest room for them. The house had separate guest quarters, which adjoined the kids' playroom, so it shared a bathroom with a room full of art supplies, trucks, trains, games. Oddly, Star, my golden retriever, started lying against the bathroom door, even if he was sprawled on top of uncomfortable toys. I thought it was so strange and figured Star was maybe just getting old, but he was protecting the boys.

The guest room also had an outside entrance, and one day my housekeeper came to my room with a strange look and said, *Miss Pamela, someone is sleeping in your bed downstairs.* I thought of Goldilocks. I couldn't imagine who it could be—it was just the boys and me in the house. I ran down and opened the door to find a strange woman with bleach-blond hair and black roots sleepily sitting up in bed, wearing my *Baywatch* bathing suit under a tattered sundress. Mumbling in broken English, she handed a letter to my housekeeper that said something like, *I'm not a lesbian, but I dream of you.*

I grabbed the boys and went outside, calling security and the police. When the police arrived, she cut her wrists with glass she'd hidden under the pillow. Blood everywhere. The poor woman had obviously been there for days. She looked homeless and hungry. I knew I'd been missing a few things—the Gucci jean jacket I loved, a pair of flip-flops, a loaf of bread I swore had been on the counter—but figured I was just absent-minded. We found it all stuffed under the bed—the smell was awful. She must have gotten the *Baywatch* bathing suit from my bedroom. It scared me to think how long she had been there or that she might have been in my room while I slept. Or near the boys ever.

The police took her away, asking me if I wanted my bathing suit back. I said, *No, that's okay,* but thanked them for asking. As it turned out, the woman was a fan, not even twenty years old, who had come all the way from France to find me. Back in her country, she'd been reported missing and was known to be troubled. She was deported back home, and her family was happy to have her back. Meanwhile, I was shaken. It was time to find a more secure spot in The Colony.

MY PARENTS HAD JUST MOVED BACK TO CANADA WHEN WE learned that my mom was having some serious health issues, to the point where they said they had to amputate her legs. I refused to believe it and flew her back to LA for a second opinion. I wanted her to meet with my doctor, Dr. Huizenga. He agreed to see her quickly and discovered that she had a disease that was caused by smoking, usually something that affects people much older than she was. A date for surgery was set.

The first surgery didn't go well, so we had to make the difficult decision of whether to immediately opt for another kind of surgery. We had known it might come to this and decided to take that leap of faith. But having the two surgeries back-to-back was not ideal and added to the risk. I felt sick, afraid we might lose her. I thought about my grandfather and what he had said about doctors. But I knew it was what my mom wanted.

Between surgeries, Mom was still in a stretcher and I was at her side. I had never seen a loved one like this, and it was scary. She was hooked up to many tubes and machines, but she was still being her funny self through the remnants of anesthesia, saying, *You really got me into a pickle this time.* I tried to be strong for her, but I was beginning to feel woozy. As they rolled her away, I must have gone *really* pale, because she said through her oxygen mask, *Figures, my daughter is going to faint. Catch her, some-one!* She was right. I woke up on the floor.

My mom's surgery went well, thankfully, and she and my dad stayed with us long after she recovered. We were grateful. Seeing her and the boys walking hand in hand along the beach filled my eyes with tears. The simple things, never to be taken for granted.

XI

While councils of grandmothers meet around the world
forecasting how to protect and nurture the planet,
the women of the future are being born today.
To be born
Is to be brave.
A calling to fully participate in earth life
In all its pain and glory.
A self-educated guess
Another kind of wisdom
A rich and exciting existence

MOST YEARS, THE BOYS AND I WENT TO THE MANSION FOR EAS-
ter. All the Playmates were invited and would bring their
families to the famous Easter egg hunt. Thousands of painted
eggs hidden all over the estate's rambling gardens and twisted
pathways. A contest that got heated, even between the adults at
times, playfully elbowing each other out of the way. Everyone
could be a kid that day. One year, when I was waiting for the
valet to bring the car, Brandon came running up to me with

Dylan in tow, yelling, *Mom!! We were just in the grotto with Marston and Cooper* [Hef's sons]. *Do you know what Hef does for a living?* I hesitated before asking, *What?* Brandon said, *He takes pictures of naked girls!!!* The boys looked disgusted and yelled, *Ewwwww.* I said, *Oh God! Let's get outta here!* We jumped into our white Range Rover, and they buckled up in their car seats as fast as they could—and we were outta there! We still laugh about it.

The girls at the Mansion looked up to me. I felt a little like the mayor. I had two beautiful sons, a career . . . Powerful men chased me, the bad boys, the unattainable ones . . . the emotionally unavailable ones, more like it. The girls would ask, *How do you do it?* My life seemed so glamorous to them, what everyone wanted and aspired to, every Playmate's dream.

On cue . . .

I met Kid Rock at a concert for charity. He was onstage with Aretha Franklin singing "R-E-S-P-E-C-T," and I was there with my friend the famed photographer David La-Chapelle. With a smirk, David pointed to the stage and said, *I think we found your next husband.* He was right.

When Kid Rock called Tommy to tell him that he loved me and wanted to marry me, Tommy told him to fuck off— and that he'd kill him. But Bob and I started dating anyway. We broke up a few times, mostly due to Tommy's interference or meddling, and I wasn't so sure I could take that next step. But eventually he got to me. He was sexy, and his talent was seductive. He lured me in, and I was helpless in the face of his rock-star advances.

I was in Saint-Tropez on a family trip with my friend Diana and our kids on her super-yacht when Bob arrived unexpect-edly, coming in on the ship's tender and hopping aboard. After spending a few days with us, he proposed. I had to return home to take the boys to Tommy, for their scheduled summer vacation, and after a slight detour, I headed back to Saint-Tropez to marry Bob.

David LaChapelle (my maid of dishonor) and I went to Vegas for my bachelorette party, along with my gorgeous, all-gay crew and Bob's security guard, Little Bear. His job was to make sure I made it back to Saint-Tropez in one piece. We ran all over the casinos—the men were all topless and I hadn't much more on than them. We were kicked out of everywhere we went. That says a lot for Vegas.

David and I haphazardly arrived at the airport without a wink of sleep. He sat me at the *Wheel of Fortune* slot machine while he went to get us drinks. Hair of the dog. I kept nodding off, then would jolt wide awake to *WHEEL. OF. FORTUNE!* People gathered around me and stared. I was used to audiences, but this was extra weird. It was like they were viewing an art installation. I had no energy to fight it. I was paralyzed, hungover, and in a state of romantic bliss.

I had taken a captain's hat from one of the boys in Vegas, and I wore it all the way to Saint-Tropez. We had to get to the boat somehow and chose the fun, least practical way. It was a comedy of errors. I'd been on plenty of WaveRunners before, but, for some reason, David and I could not stay on one together. We kept falling off, laughing like crazy people, and it was all captured on film. The word was out—the European tabloids were all over us, circling us with arrows, saying, "This is not her fiancé." Photos of me in David's lap, with a glass of champagne spilling in my hand, wearing my hat and bikini. Even at the wedding, the minister was confused and tried to marry us. David walked me down the aisle to "give me away" and had to stop the minister and say, *Not* me*! She's marrying him!* Bob didn't enjoy this and made it clear that *he* was my husband.

After the wedding, I wanted to jump off the boat in my punky Heatherette wedding dress, and David was egging me on, laughing. *Do it!* Then Bob stopped me and said, *No!* As I straddled the edge, I looked at them both. I remember how I felt in that moment: conflicted. But reluctantly chose to obey my new husband.

We returned to the beach to find a sea of cameras, at least a hundred of them. Bob was on the turntables at Nikki Beach—he is a super-talented DJ and always entertaining. After a few days of celebration, we rested up and went home to our family.

Bob didn't appreciate my close relationship with David. He also didn't believe David was really gay. David and I have always been very close, soulmates in some ways. I'd found someone who accepted me, full stop, and nurtured and instigated the artistic side of me like no one else. We'd watch documentaries and talk about art. When we walked in anywhere, people knew it was about to get wild. We'd dance around in our underwear—or less. Hanging from the chandeliers.

While reading Patti Smith's memoir *Just Kids,* when she discussed her relationship with Robert Mapplethorpe, it reminded me of David and I, in some ways. But the Chateau Marmont was our Chelsea Hotel. Together our life always seemed to be more colorful, unique, fun, and twisted. Yet there was an innocence about it, something childlike. Between us, there were no filters. We could be ourselves completely. It was a kind of love that was based on acceptance and had nothing to do with time or space.

My boys saved me. I lived a normal family life but also had this wild, artistic group around me, where everything was like living in a version of one of David's photographs. We were connected in a way no one else could come close to, my own Factory crew. *Warhol would've loved you,* David said. His first job was at Studio 54, working for Andy and *Interview* magazine. He was a street kid in New York at the time, and I was searching for myself in LA. When David met Pamela . . .

The first time we shot together, for *Details* magazine, we connected instantly. David asked if I'd like to pose as a blow-up doll in a toy store window. I said of course I would. He was surprised at how easy it was to get me to do it. But I was up for anything. I just trusted him inherently. David would call to tell me one of our covers was out, and I'd just reply, *Great,* and move on to discuss something else. He'd ask, *Do you want to see it?* And I'd tell him, *Not really.* He'd laugh and tell me that I was the only person he had ever met who acted this way. *The least ambitious person on the planet.*

It was sincere
Archetypal
My life was pure Fate.
My humble offering to the world.

David directed me in a visual video installation for *The Red Piano,* a live Elton John show at Caesars Palace in Vegas. We filmed a piece that was projected behind Elton as he played, my image blown up on twelve-hundred-foot screens, pole-dancing to "The Bitch Is Back." Before the shoot, I had never pole-danced before, but I trusted David's vision—and knew we'd have fun together. As we were filming, David giggled while blowing bubbles at me using a bubble machine from behind the camera, as I tried to be both sexy and smolderingly focused. I'm not sure why I felt the need to swing around as fast as I could—the extensions were flying out of my hair. In the end, I just fell to the floor and rolled around, feeling the burn through my legs, laughing and crying out loud, *Lactic acid!* Luckily, David got what he needed for the film in one very long take—and thank God, because once was enough for me.

I loved that I could be so open and wildly uninhibited with David and our circle. To be surrounded by free spirits. Jesus "Half Animal" Villa, a world-record-making acrobat and the star of Cirque du Soleil's *Zumanity*. Guy Laliberté, fire-eater and founder of Cirque du Soleil, who took in Jesus like a son. Luca "Pizza" Pizzaroni, a talented artist and photographer, who shot a bunch for David. Luca's book, *End Commercial,* saw beauty in the things people walk by and take for granted. Bambini, a handsome, poetic modern dancer who also starred in some of the Elton pieces. We liked to keep it in the family. Elton said he loved David and he loved me, but the two of us together were dangerous.

BOB AND I STARTED SPENDING MORE TIME IN DETROIT, HIS HOME-town. We had our big family wedding there, where Bob Seger and Hank Williams Jr. sang for us. Our life in Detroit was full of music. I took for granted all those nights with Hank, ZZ Top, Uncle Kracker, Eminem, and Bob's band. To be around such talent was inspiring. It was a true rock-and-roll lifestyle, gritty and soulful. Detroit had an energy all its own.

Bob had taken on a lot with me and two boys—he was really great to them and had a young son himself. On Bob's ranch, just outside the city, there were always adventures. They rode dirt bikes, snowmobiles, and horses. Bob's friend Chelios played hockey for the Detroit Red Wings, and for Dylan's fourth birthday party, the boys skated with the team at practice. They played golf with John Daly, who could famously open a beer can by hitting a golf ball off the top to crack it open, and they passed a football with Peyton Manning. The boys loved Bob. He made a huge effort.

At times, our differences were so apparent, I'd leave to take time to think. Then I'd have Mr. Ahmet Ertegun, the founder of Atlantic Records and legend, call me on Bob's behalf and try to convince me to give him another chance. I'd arrive in New York for work, and there they would both be, sitting in the lobby of the St. Regis, at the piano, playing and singing "A Song for You" by Donny Hathaway. Or another one of our songs, "For Your Precious Love." It's a dirty game when a man can just sing you a song—you can't help but cave to his abilities. His secret weapon. And I fell for it every time.

I wanted to be back in Malibu, though. I had rented a small house on Escondido Beach, but it was tiny for the five of us, so Bob found us a more suitable home on Point Dume and bought it. We were about to move in, until the premiere of *Borat*. The screening at Ron and Kelly Meyer's house didn't go well. Lots of important industry people were there—Steven Spielberg, Rick Rubin, Laird Hamilton and his wife, Gabby Reece. I didn't tell Bob I was in the movie, because I wanted to surprise him. I forgot about the part in the film that referenced the "sex tape." Bob stormed out, calling me a whore and worse. He was embarrassed, and his reaction was not thought through. Laird yelled, *Don't get mad at Superwoman when she busts out her cape!* After I chased Bob to his car, he peeled out, leaving me there alone. I turned back and apologized, then asked if anyone could give me a ride home. When I walked in, Bob was smashing a photo on the wall. He said he was sick of waking up to a picture of me and David LaChapelle every day. But it wasn't me and David—it was Marilyn Monroe and Bert Stern.

We broke up. I didn't stay in touch with Bob.

But as bad luck had it, I was asked to present an award to Kanye West at MTV's Video Music Awards. I saw Bob on the red carpet and he looked at me and said, *Look what the cat dragged in.* Then I saw Tommy. He entered from another way—kind of sneaking in and taking a seat—and when I slipped past him to sit down, Tommy pulled me onto his lap. He was sitting next to the magician Criss Angel, and I asked Criss if he could make Tommy disappear. Bob saw the whole thing and was fuming from his seat across from us. After I presented the award to Kanye, Alicia Keys started singing her new single "No One," and at the lyrics "Everything's gonna be alright," Tommy and Bob dove at each other. Fists were flying, and the whole thing ended up on live TV. I walked out, and Alicia didn't miss a beat, kept on singing. It was a setup. MTV must have been thrilled. I told the press waiting outside that we were bamboozled.

Boys will be boys.

XII

With closed eyes, I hear their shuffling footsteps
Good morning, sweethearts—
Is it breakfast time?
Sweet, soft voices vibrating my ear to wake me up gently.
Whispering,
Mom, Mom, Mom—
We're going to go check the waves.
Eyes still closed,
I'd sing, Okay.

Time to get up
and make lunches—
while they decide if it's worth surfing before school.

BUILDING MY PLACE IN THE COLONY IN MALIBU LITERALLY TOOK
years—and everything I had. When the construction became
too much, we moved to a trailer I'd bought in Paradise Cove,
which was the best purchase I'd ever made. While The Colony
was a playground for starlets, retired movie stars, writers, musi-

cians, mistresses, and artists, Paradise Cove was home to firemen, police officers, soul surfers, and their families—the real Malibu.

The boys preferred the Cove to The Colony. It was their heaven—surfing every day, racing in golf carts. It was like *Stand by Me* on the beach. It didn't hurt that there were lots of pretty girls around their age. More "tomboys" who weren't spoiled, like you might expect to find in LA. The kids there were athletic, fun, and loved the ocean and skateboarding more than being on their phones or computers—good kids, with more hands-on parents.

Our trailer was perched on a cliff over the water—the great Pacific Ocean stretched out in front of us. Near all the best surf spots, Old Joe's, Westward, down to Zuma. Our home was the epitome of shabby chic—distressed wood floors, vaulted white ceilings. Lots of rugs, blankets, bunk beds, cozy white denim couches, and a few chandeliers. We made it our own. And we felt safe there. The park had a security gate, and our trailer was gated and private. Though all the neighborhood kids had the code to get in—if not, they jumped the fence. Inside the yard was an outdoor shower surrounded by a line of surfboards and boogie boards, a Zodiac, and the golf cart, plugged in and ready to go. We had a Jacuzzi in a garden full of flowers mixed in with tomato plants and herbs—proudly Provençal. All the kids would pile in the Jacuzzi, even if they were still in their wetsuits, to warm up after a cold surf.

Just after the crack of dawn, the boys would drive the golf cart, covered in surfboard stickers, to the lookout, to check out how their favorite breaks looked that day. Then they'd zoom off to collect their crew: Conrad, Ryder, Biggie, then Boogie. Conrad was the oldest and hardest to wake up, so Dylan, who never wanted to be late, would climb in the window and shake him to get him up. Eventually, they would all come back to the trailer, excitedly chatting about which breaks looked best, me with coffee mug in hand, slowly waking up. I preferred my own strong barista-style coffee to Starbucks—fun to make, and less waste. Our hideous Kangen water filter sat on the counter attached to our sink (but then no need for bottled water), alongside a Pasquini espresso machine. The boys would fight over who got to make me coffee—grinding the beans, pressing the espresso, and preparing the perfect almond or oat milk foam, presented to me in the mug of their choice, usually a fun novelty one that the boys had bought me, WORLD'S BEST MOM or SUPERMOM emblazoned on the side.

Wetsuits, towels, boards and wax, a change of clothes, and we were off. We'd pile into my early nineties Range Rover Classic or '66 Scout, depending on which car the kids wanted to take or whichever one started that day. I loved my vintage trucks, had started to collect them. It seemed I always had a vehicle in the shop getting refurbished, from small boats like my kids' Zodiac and my Chris-Craft to an assortment of hot rods and Airstreams. When I was on *VIP*, I had a thirty-three-foot classic Airstream on the set—pink ghost flames on the side and a license plate that read "Hos Up" (as a play on Ice-T's *Pimps Up*). I hated to let go of any of the vehicles—they all had personalities and were labors of love. But they accumulated, and someone always made me an offer I couldn't refuse. I had a knack for spotting the ones with soul and character—now old Broncos and Scouts are all the rage. I smile when I think about that—I was ahead of my time.

I'd usually drive the kids to Zuma Beach, a pristine stretch of long, rolling waves where you can easily park on the side of the Pacific Coast Highway. While they went out, I would go for a walk with Jojo Rock Star (our beloved retriever at the time)—there was always room for Jojo in the truck, usually on top of the boys. Then I'd watch my boys surf from the beach, or from the truck's front seat on colder days. I'd call in our order of breakfast burritos (no beans) from Lily's—the best in Malibu—picking them up as soon as she opened. By eight, I'd have to start calling the boys in from the water. It was a struggle—they would always negotiate, want more time, me yelling, *COME ON*, over the roar of the waves. I'd say, *LET'S GO!* only to see Dylan, with that little-shit, mischievous smile, paddle out one more time. Finally, I'd stand on the truck bumper and hold up and shake the bag of burritos to get them to come in. That always worked.

Somehow, we were never late to school. The boys would quickly change out of their wetsuits and rinse off at the outdoor beach showers, then pull on shorts, shoes, and hoodies. They'd eat their burritos in the car like madmen, passing back and forth a big jug of orange juice and laughing about how the surf was and who did what out there. School was just a five-minute drive, and in a flash, they'd open the car door, piling out in shambles, hair long and wet, shaking it out, like dogs do, just as the first bell was ringing. We'd say I-love-yous with kisses and hugs, and with that, they'd run with their backpacks into the building. With a morning's surf in them, the teachers would have more focused students in my boys. They were already worn out and ready to learn.

I had my own routines, a creature of habit. I would then take my walk around Pepperdine University, a hike with spectacular views of Malibu. A brisk walk with fresh air is always better than going to a gym. One day, the school minister saw me walking and asked to join me. I had just helped to raise money for the lights on the baseball field, and he wanted to thank me. I had seen him around Malibu and thought he really did seem like a holy man. There was something so calm and serene about him. As we were walking together, he began to tell me that God wanted him to help me—that's why he had approached. He was drawn to start a conversation with me. Truth was, I loved talking to him and trusted him immediately. We walked together like this for years. Our conversations fed my curiosity. He told me that I needed "fences," more boundaries. He would counsel me as we walked up and down the hills, through olive and coral trees. I admired the university's dedication to using mainly native vegetation and protecting its natural wetlands. It was a healthy hike and a real challenge to do in the always-warm, Mediterranean-style climate of Malibu.

The minister became a dear friend, and kind of a therapist. I told him everything, confessed deep secrets. His advice always came without judgment. He was an angel, I thought, through his inspiring ministry God's Love Never Fails. He had helped so many, a godsend, and it was a shock to all when we lost him unexpectedly. He died while reading his Bible on the beach. On our last walk, I had noticed his breath was labored, his forehead beaded with sweat. I asked him if he was okay and told him we didn't have to walk that day, but he said, *No, let's keep going.* He died of an enlarged heart—that made sense to me.

A life of selfless service
Mission accomplished
Not one moment is guaranteed.

I think of Maurice often. I still walk the same path every time I'm in Malibu, and I feel his presence there. I believe nobody really dies.

Our lives in the Cove felt so bohemian and free—a spiritual cleansing. The boys and I played host to so many eclectic friends and visitors over the years. Vivienne Westwood and her husband, Andreas Kronthaler, once visited. Vivienne and I met while petitioning for Indigenous activist Leonard Peltier's release from prison, and she invited me to attend one of her fashion shows in Paris. I spent more time reading the manifesto she left on the chair than admiring the clothes. When we met backstage, I went on and on about her poetry and mention of fairy tales. She instantly said, *I don't have to draw you a map.* We became friends just like that, and I went on to appear in multiple fashion campaigns for her and Andreas. Vivienne has a profound influence on anyone she meets—or has time for. Later, when Brandon was eighteen, he interned for Vivienne in London. It was an unconventional but perfect education: she would send him to museums, and when he returned, she'd ask him which painting he'd save in a fire, sending him back over and over until he knew. Brandon learned all aspects of the business, working in design, PR, even retail at her famous shop on King's Road.

By then, Brandon was old enough for me to get him a membership to the Playboy Club in London, so he had somewhere to go if he needed anything. I told the girls there to keep an eye on him. They most certainly did, with no complaints from Brandon.

Vivienne is unbelievably special—real, raw, no filter. A creator of punk, in style and attitude. When she and Andreas came with Juergen Teller to my tiny trailer in Malibu, all we had was an extra blow-up mattress, because we hadn't moved in properly yet, but no one was fussy, no need for fancy. Together, we all watched the inauguration of President Obama. We were all so full of hope. Later, we made spaghetti with Queens of the Stone Age, who came by for the shoot and a visit. My neighbors thought I had crazy relatives over all the time and that we liked to take odd family pictures. Juergen took photos of me as I was skateboarding in a pink couture wedding dress. We took eclectic photos in the trailer park's laundromat and on the trail to the beach. Vivienne loved that I had so many books and was an avid reader—she always said, *If you read, you'll never be boring, and you'll always have a job*—so when she found a volume of Plato on my bedside table, she insisted Juergen take photos of me reading it leaning up against a tree, sitting on a park bench, rolling with it in the sand.

The artist Richard Prince also visited me at the trailer. We walked holding hands down the trail and the beach, he in his white Speedo, and talked about everything, from art to religion to porn. He told me how he had Coke cans hanging in the doorway of his naughty theater, so you would never be caught in the act, you could hear before anyone turned the corner. We laughed like crazy, especially when we tried to come up with a scheme to meet the notoriously cantankerous artist Mr. Heizer, who lived close to Vegas. He was an earth mover, working on his masterpiece, *City*. I'd been curious about him, and Richard said we should make a short film—drive the Airstream out there and film what might transpire. We imagined being run off the property, or, best case, being yelled at but being taken in to appreciate the work.

Werner Herzog was calling me at this time, too. His films felt raw, intense, a unique, driven viewpoint. From *Cave of Forgotten Dreams,* his documentary on French cave paintings, to *Fitzcarraldo,* he was fearless, and he had the admiration of our mutual friend Ed Ruscha. I remember Ed begging me to *please* work with Herzog—he thought it would be a brilliant pairing. Unfortunately, Werner's project for me fell apart. It happens. It was the thought that counted to me—I loved being on his radar at all. Werner was the one who reminded me to not audition for anyone. He said it was a waste of time, and that if a director couldn't see in me what he saw, they weren't worth working with. I took his advice to heart.

Our trailer was a hot spot—people were drawn to it, and that made me proud. I took in a lot of kids over the years, some of whom became like family. I made breakfast for all. My famous waffles. My boys would just let me know how many friends were coming, and I'd get to making stacks of them. Kids in the park knew they could come to me with anything. I saw myself in some of them, and I wanted to support them with an open heart, lots of food and love. Like what had been done for me in my early life. Not everyone was as lucky as my boys—they knew that, and we'd make sure we helped others when they needed it.

For me, Paradise Cove was a place to simplify. A valuable, minimalist idea. We cleaned house once a year, and all the money went to charity. It felt good to start fresh. We sold our odds and ends to benefit my foundation, the Pamela Anderson Foundation, which gives to those on the front lines who are risking their lives every day for vulnerable people, animals, and the environment. Our yard sales were scrappy and creative to draw attention. We had a few friends walking around in chicken bikinis, holding anti-KFC signage, with tricked-out lemonade stands that looked like an art installation, a giant graffitied sign saying NICE LEMONS above it. One lemonade stand raised $30,000 for the California Wildlife Center. A friend from The Colony was so impressed, he said he'd match what the kids made, so we doubled it. Good intentions validated. And we had fun doing it.

XIII

Gamble everything for love, if you are a true human being . . .
Half-heartedness doesn't reach into majesty.
—RUMI

I WAS OFFERED A MAGIC SHOW IN VEGAS, A THREE-MONTH STINT
as a magician's assistant for Hans Klok. My agent thought I
shouldn't do it, which meant I said, *Yes, of course, I'll do it,* without
hesitation. Always in rebellion. But it sounded like fun. And
even better—I hoped David could shoot the billboard. I was
always thinking visually and looking for ways to get my creative
crew involved.

The show was a thrill. My favorite parts of the act were
when I was levitated and when I had fire spikes driven through
me. It was dangerous, but my double-jointed shoulders and
flexibility came in handy. I loved being able to perform in front
of a live audience. One heartbeat—the crowd was just as much
a part of the experience as the performers. I realized how com-
fortable I was onstage, maybe even more than anywhere else.

The whole atmosphere of the show appealed to me—creatives of all sorts, coordinated mayhem. While I was getting my makeup and hair done in the dressing room, I hired a professional clown to teach me how to make balloon animals, never wanting to waste time. Part of the fun was to make them really fast—like magic, *ta-da!* They would turn out pretty interesting—and always somewhat deformed. I'd tape them to the wall over my bed, or to my friends' hotel doors as a welcome. As they deflated and shriveled, they got even better. Strange, almost conceptual pieces.

Always good
to have skills—
As many as you can
to keep in your pocket.
Something
to fall back on—

After the shows, my wonderful, supportive gang would visit me backstage. Amy Winehouse, Thierry Mugler, and well-known drag queens Elaine Lancaster and Lady Bunny. And when they all sat in the front row, people complained they couldn't see past the hair. My dressing room was a scene, mirrors on the ceiling, the walls graffitied by street artist Marcus Suarez, and always an inch of glitter on the floor. My longtime friend the boxer and poker player Rick Salomon would also stop by from time to time. He always had eyes for me, but I thought of him only as a friend.

I was only in Vegas on show days and would fly back and forth four times a week. Even after the craziest run of shows and late flights, I'd take the boys to school. At drop-off I'd work as a volunteer, ushering kids from their cars. Occasionally, I'd catch a reflection of myself in a car window and realize I was covered in glitter, my eyes still blackened by last night's show's eyeliner, smudging down my cheeks, hair teased into a scary mess.

I rarely looked in the mirror in the mornings—
I'd laugh,
though.
I'd think—
Glitter doesn't make me a bad mom—
The state
of some of those cars was worse—
sandwiches jammed in backseat pockets,
empty chip bags, dirty socks, empty water bottles—
Everyone alive is a mess.
We are all just doing the best we can.

When I was staying in Vegas, I was given the top floor of Planet Hollywood. Marcus stayed with me to keep me company. We made it fun for the boys and their friends when they'd come, creating treasure hunts around the room. We built a track for electric cars that ran down the hallway, weaving in and out of the rooms.

If anyone fell asleep before us, we tied them up like in *Gulliver's Travels* and built potato chip sculptures on them. We'd call room service with bizarre questions—*What's more expensive? Half clams on the whole shell, or whole clams on the half shell?* We'd Saranwrap the doors shut and make picket signs that said things like,

INCIDENTALLY, I HAVE TO PAY FOR INCIDENTALS. OR STEPHEN HAWKING IS A KLEPTO, because things of mine went missing all the time—shoes, jewelry, bags, cash—and we joked there must be a black hole somewhere in the room. To this day, I have no idea where those things went. I was starting to get used to people stealing from me. I just thought, If someone had to steal, they must need it more than me. Liars and thieves aplenty.

The truth was, I really did not like Vegas—but Vegas loved me. I had my own slot machines and poker chips with David LaChapelle images on them at the Palms. They would even take the "L" out if I was in residence, so the sign up on high read PAMS. Chuck Zito of the Hells Angels once drove me through the casino on his Harley for a special event, which was unheard of—not least because we had to get Chuck a weekend pass, since he'd been banned from Vegas for who knows what. Chuck is an angel in my eyes—he's always had my back.

Lots of hotels were pitching me shows at the time, so when Steve Wynn called me in for a meeting, I thought he was going to do the same and ask me to perform at his hotel. But instead, he gave me a stern warning. He said, *Pamela, I like you—you're a good girl, a good mom—but you need to get rid of the people around you.* Then he went on to say that he would love me to do a show at his hotel someday, but right now I was a liability. I took this to heart. It felt like a sign from the universe, confirmation of what I knew was a fun but ultimately destructive environment. I didn't agree to another run with the magic show or take any more projects on. It was time to get out of Las Vegas and reset.

ALWAYS A WAY OUT . . .

Marcus and my driver, Errol, had gotten themselves into trouble while we were in Vegas. They were playing blackjack in my room and ended up owing Rick a couple hundred thousand dollars. Rick said that he would forgive the debt . . . if I married him. I thought he was joking. And then he upped the ante, he threw in that I'd have to have sex with him, right then. Calling his bluff, I said, *Okay!* Rick was a handsome guy, quite the character, and we'd known each other for years—he'd been chasing me ever since I first met him. So I called him into the bedroom, lay down on the floor. I teasingly pulled my dress up over my head, naked from the neck down, and said, muffled from under my sweater, *Let's do this.* He laughed and pulled my sweater away from my face, looked deep into my eyes, and kissed me hard. We made love right there. It was thrilling and unexpected.

It also led to something more serious. Rick and I had an undeniable connection, and I knew that he adored me. Though his ask to me may have been bold, he was actually a shy person. Extremely bright, an observer, but also a bit maniacal. Scary, interesting, tough, funny. I still can't believe I said yes and followed through. We got married between magic shows, with his two daughters and my two sons present. Our kids got along great and still do.

> *Even with my past experiences*
> *I never gave up.*
> *I wanted to be married*
> *I wanted to feel safe*
> *I wanted a family for my boys.*

Seeking harmony in inharmonious places
Was just my curse—and my style.

A few months later, my assistant found what he thought was a crack pipe in the Christmas tree. People had warned me that Rick was a serious addict, but I'd never seen that side of him. It seemed like an exaggeration. Rick insists to this day that my assistant planted the pipe in the tree to break us up. But I couldn't risk it. We had the marriage annulled and remained friends.

With all this madness, I decided to shed the past and thought I might do that by changing my look—a new start. I started dressing more like French film stars, like Bardot in the movie *Contempt*. Striped skirts and cardigans, ballet flats. Fellini sunglasses, like Anita Ekberg. I even cut my hair into a sixties-style pixie cut reminiscent of Jean Seberg.

Living cinematically
And dramatically
Is what
I have always aspired to
Why not?
Inspired by filmic women—
Gena Rowlands in A Woman Under the Influence
*   by Cassavetes.*
Ava Gardner in Night of the Iguana.
Julianne Moore in Safe,
and in A Single Man.
I dream I am the woman in Valentino . . .
Desperate, alone, glamorous,
misunderstood.

Wanting to be loved,
admired.
Never the right man . . .

Women are really not respected
To this day.
That's why we need humor,
style, stamina, art.

I did a photo shoot for *Vanity Fair* with Mamie Van Doren. The photographer, Ali Mahdavi, was brilliant, hanging orbs to light our faces like the starlets of the fifties, almost in homage to George Hurrell. We were styled by Tom Ford, who was guest editor that month. Tom came into my dressing area and took scissors to the front of my dress, ripping it from bottom to top, till I was bare naked in front of him. He eyed me up and down, then pulled the dress off me and threw it to the ground, asking the seamstress to get to work on it. Then he put me in a nude Thierry Mugler corset from the archives and started pulling the strings, pulling and pulling. He finally stopped and turned me around, looked into my eyes, and said, *You have NO organs, you must never leave the house without a corset.* Then he snapped his fingers to demand his measuring tape. He turned me again and continued to pull me to seventeen inches. We both gasped. He said he could go farther, but I might break in half. The seamstress helped me back into the creamy white dress, sewing it directly onto me. *Like Marilyn Monroe.* Pure elegance. He said it suited me. Tom just knew glamour.

WHILE I WAS ON A WORK TRIP TO MOSCOW, I GOT A CALL FROM a handsome businessman, an art collector I had a fascination with. An Oscar Wilde type. He spent part of his time in Russia but told me he was out of the country. Still, he asked where I was staying and what my plans were. I told him I had to work in the morning, but then I'd be at the Pushkin Museum at two P.M. I enjoyed going to museums alone, incognito. An escape. I went to the museum and was admiring its great works. As he crossed my mind, I turned a corner, and there he fucking was. We both took a long, deep breath, drinking each other in. Such a thrill, from head to toe. Electric. He gave me a quick lesson in Bronzino, his low, knowing voice so sensual. He was mysterious, smart, sophisticated. A visionary, an activist for art and animals.

We walked arm in arm back to my hotel, through the snow, next to the looming, deep-red buildings, his security team trailing us fifty feet behind. At the hotel entrance, he kissed me politely, and we said goodbye. Then he disappeared into the night. He was returning to his plane, off to London—or to Italy, where he rescued wolves, or to one of his four elephant sanctuaries in different parts of Africa. We always had our wild moments, our encounters. At his house in the countryside, once, in a long gold evening gown in the shower. Or a romantic dinner for two by candlelight, when I removed my faux fur to reveal a sheer lace Coco de Mer dress that left nothing to the imagination. We enjoyed each other's boldness.

Magical moments like these—
Captured,
Stored in memory—

Are the alive ones—
the ones that get you through
the years, the months, the days.
I plant the seeds
And wait.
Good lovers are
few and far between.

XIV

The human spirit
has always been an interest of mine—
and my relationships prove that.
Some as curious
as me.

I ALWAYS FELT HONORED WHEN I RECEIVED MESSAGES OF SUP-
port from the glamorous bombshell women of other eras. Bri-
gitte Bardot called me her "daughter." We have worked on
many animal rights campaigns together but have never met
in person. And Raquel Welch gave me advice on men. *Be with*
someone unexpected, she said. I think I took that too much to heart
in my later years. Ursula Andress called me her favorite, and
Jane Fonda told me, *Don't let them do to you what they did to me.*

Media can be a bitch.
A weapon,
or used for good.

The most important thing to me, after being a mom, was my deep passion for animals and the environment. Activism fit alongside my career naturally. I've spent years campaigning for PETA and many other like-minded organizations. This work brought some very special people into my life. One such angel was my dear friend Sam Simon, co-developer of *The Simpsons* and a fellow animal activist. Sam had terminal cancer when I started to visit him. We'd "work out" together, passing balloons back and forth. I'd make him my famous balloon animals that always ended up missing a leg or a head, just to make him smile. He loved them. In return, he'd draw pictures of me, caricatures à la *The Simpsons,* in blue Sharpie.

Sam and I shared common interests. He was very funny, just a joy to be around. Our relationship became deeply affectionate very quickly. We had endless discussions about things that were important to us, like saving animals and art. His mother had been a collector who owned a gallery, so he had inherited an incredible collection and had bought a lot of art himself—a beautiful Rodin sculpture and other pieces by Benton, Ruscha, Vargas, and Ramos. I would bring by emerging artists, people he wanted to meet from my orbit, and we'd talk late into the night.

Sam wanted to go out on the town. He didn't want to stay locked away inside. Against doctor's orders, we went to Sean Penn's gala for Haiti. But Sam was on a lot of meds and started heckling President Clinton during his speech, and hitting on David Spade's girlfriend, who was seated next to us at our table. Security was not happy, and we were asked to leave. It was time to get him out of there. It was his birthday, and on the way home, I surprised him with something illegal . . . I commissioned a graffiti artist friend of mine to tag a building on Sunset Boulevard, a scene of the two of us, done *Simpsons* style. He was in tears, just blown away. Even though it was painted over the next day, it can never be erased.

Sam and I both supported Sea Shepherd, an ocean conservation organization. I was the international chair for years, and they put Sam's name on the side of a ship—which meant he'd donated millions. Sea Shepherd remained faithful to Sam—and maintains the boat in his honor, to this day.

It's a privilege to be so close to someone so close to death—every second is precious, honest. Near the end, Sam started to see people in the room with me, behind me. But there was nobody there. He would swear at them and say, *NO! Get the fuck out!* I would tell him calmly, *It's okay, they don't bother me.*

Every time we said goodbye, it was harder and harder to leave, because I never knew if I'd see him again.

It was crushing when Sam passed. I was asked to speak at his funeral, and I remember as they lowered him into the grave, my phone went off, breaking the sad silence. My ringtone was George Michael's "Freedom!" I frantically tried to shut it off, apologizing . . . I have to believe Sam had something to do with that. He was always one to lighten a mood.

ANY TIME I TRAVELED FOR WORK, ANYWHERE IN THE WORLD, I would research the pressing animal rights issue in the area and try to act on it, to use my influence for good. In my travels, I've met with world leaders and spoken on issues far and wide with promising results. I've found it's most important to be thoughtful and intentional with your actions. That means advocating with respect, instead of being the typical Westerner who always wants to impose their annoying points of view and not-always-shared opinions on others.

I traveled to Tokyo for twenty-four hours to present an MTV Award and had read about the tragic situation in Taiji with the dolphins—a bloody hunt for aquarium theme parks all over the world. I was planning a small act of protest: I was going to wear a T-shirt that read STOP THE HUNT when I walked on-stage. The authorities firmly told me not to do so. I thought a lot about it. It wasn't that I caved to their demands, but I chose not to wear it, thinking there might be a more clever and impactful way to deal with the issue. I had something better up my sleeve. I searched for local passionate activists. I decided then and there that, whenever possible, to support organizations that are work-ing inside a country, those who are aware of the culture and the unique sensitivities. There are many ways to navigate. I've found that being sensitive and respectful is effective everywhere I go. There are kindhearted people all over the world, willing to do the hard work in their own backyard.

When we think of the rain forest, we might think only of the Amazon—the lungs of the Earth—but our mini ecosystems are important as well, and it's up to us to try to understand their complexities and do all we can to keep them healthy and thriving. My home, Vancouver Island, is a rain forest. I've got-ten more involved in my own community projects, while still supporting Green Party efforts worldwide and Indigenous and First Nations' family and culture initiatives.

My trips to fight against deforestation in places like El Sal-vador, Honduras, and Haiti were illuminating. Gerry and I went to plant trees around the world and supported efforts to find alternatives to slash-and-burn agriculture, working with the Inga Foundation. Along the way, we met bird-watchers, nature lovers, and fellow animal lovers who asked me how to get more involved. I love the idea of voluntourism—see the world and help where you can, based on local needs. More giving than taking. All we need is empathy, stamina of spirit, and a willingness to never give up.

On-the-ground activism has always opened my eyes. Visiting Haiti after the earthquake in 2010 broke my heart. Haiti is the poorest country in the Western Hemisphere, devastated by natural disasters and corruption, but it's only an hour from Miami. That always confused me—that it's so close, but so far out of our consciousness and minds. It's criminally selfish to turn a blind eye. What I saw there will never leave me—everything in rubble, people searching for survivors and finding dead bodies under the rocks. Widespread chaos and emotional devastation. One small thing I knew to do was to bring cold beer to volunteers at camps who worked tirelessly to set up tents and rehome people who had lost everything. This is when I started to support Sean Penn's nonprofit, at the time called J/P Haitian Relief Organization, and now called CORE.

I created my foundation, the Pamela Anderson Foundation, decades ago, to be a bridge between the generous people I knew and the guerrilla NGOs and the hard-core activists risking their lives every day. We also lent a hand in producing documentaries that shone a light on helpful initiatives around the world. I've been fortunate enough to share what I've learned from some of the best. Like Captain Paul Watson, who wisely teaches us, *If the oceans die, we die.*

I feel the ocean in my own way—
Through my fingers but also
running through my veins—
The captain says
To be alive
is to be of humble service—

It's usually those without a cause
who are the angriest ones.
Projecting their shame, blame,
And an unfortunate lack of interest in the world—
Apathy is a sickness.
But there are many angels in the world.

A frequent partner in crime was Dan Mathews, former vice president of PETA. We worked together on endless edgy and provocative campaigns protecting animal rights—battling the giants over and over, and winning.

When I traveled for work, he was always my plus-one, ready and eager to provoke. I was often invited to speak at Oxford or Cambridge about wide-ranging issues, and once invited him along to discuss veganism to a host of students at the debate union halls. The energy was exhilarating. To cut the heaviness, I grabbed the mic and joked, *I've never worn a tassel on my hat before,* to a rolling sea of hysterics. Combining humor and hard-hitting messages has been my key to being a successful activist. Broadening perspectives, debating, sharing ideas. Change can be a chain reaction, especially when engaging young, hungry, receptive minds.

When I joined PETA
and helped to create animal
welfare laws
where there were none,
I spoke often
and intimately
with world leaders,
and other government officials.
NGOs used me to get in the door—
By whatever means necessary—
But,
once in the door, I'd
surprise people
with even more voluptuous
sentences
A virile engagement
they hadn't bargained for . . .

When
you have nothing to live up to—
you can't disappoint—
People whispered
I might be "genius"
If I could form a full sentence—
Utter shock—
that I might be
educated, well-read,
and prepared for the causes
I was fighting for—
and sincerely held close to my heart.

Sometimes all they wanted
was an autograph—
or a kiss on the cheek—
I wanted laws to be changed.

We both got what we wanted . . .
More often than not.

I was invited to the Kremlin to speak on animal cruelty and environmental issues, endangered tigers and bears, even saving Antarctica. Together, we had some terrific success stopping the hideous Canadian baby seal hunt, where 95 percent of seal products were exported to Russia. I implored the men sitting across from me at the table, the ones in power who could make real-time decisions, to make laws and implement them, right then and there. I called for the country to stop the illegal capture of whales, which were being sold to aquariums, mostly in China, and demanded the release of the twelve beluga whales who had been kidnapped from the ocean and were being held captive in small pens in a rural area, where no one thought they'd be found. Whales usually swim a hundred miles a day, so when they are penned, they get deathly cold. These belugas were experiencing hypothermia. I shared photos, horrific undercover footage we had gathered—it was an embarrassment to Russia. Finally, the belugas were released from the "whale jail," after an international outcry. And the whales survived the release, thankfully. Russia also doubled down, making it illegal to transport endangered species by air, sea, or land through any part of the country. The trip was a huge success. My Russian roots were proud.

While in Moscow, I paid a visit to an orphanage, some hours outside of the city. This wasn't one of the "Hollywood orphanages," but a real and struggling institution that housed children of every age—from babies to teenagers, including kids with disabilities. Most had been given up or had been found living on the street. Two ladies, "babushkas," ran the entire place, caring for the kids, doing the cleaning and cooking. The children were only allowed to stay until they turned sixteen, at which point they'd have to go back out onto the street to survive somehow. The thought of that struggle affected me deeply. I spoke to several of these "graduating" teens and asked them what they wanted to be when they grew up. Their big dreams were always humble jobs—it was eye-opening. I gave each of the teens a gift to help them on their way—a sewing machine for a young woman who wanted to be a seamstress, a toolbox for a boy who wanted to build furniture. I offered to repaint the institute, to replace the lead paint, and to give them a washer/dryer—but they refused, saying they had to be extremely careful about what they accepted, fearing the government might cut them off if they took large contributions. When it was time to leave, a little boy clutched my leg. It was so hard, so heartbreaking. There is so much need in the world for understanding.

I later went to Moscow on another trip to attend fundraising luncheons for the Russian chapter of the International Fund for Animal Welfare, of which I was on the board. A few wealthy families were considering giving support and asked if we could meet to further discuss. The drive was long and I was jet-lagged, not having adjusted to the time difference, and I drifted off in the car. When I woke up, we had arrived at an estate, where armed guards with machine guns lined the driveway. We were introduced to our host, who preferred to speak in Russian, but there was an interpreter, who sat next to me. They had an incredible vegan spread. It was hard not to notice the staff of beautiful women and men who served us. We discussed the plight of the whales in detail. He listened half-heartedly—bored and more interested in giving me a tour of his house, making it clear he wanted me to come with him and his team alone. I insisted that I take one of my people.

We stepped into a modern elevator, with just a white gate around us—it was otherwise transparent. On descent, it revealed what looked like an underground city. It's vivid in my memory. We walked by an office with large white telephones, followed by another room that had a dentist's chair. He joked that he hated going to the dentist. I was wearing impossibly high Louboutin shoes, which tapped loudly as we walked down the white marble hallway. I was focused on trying not to slip. We passed several more rooms, with small windows on the doors, like cells, I thought. I joked that if anyone was missing, I would know where they were. That didn't get a laugh. I preferred to think that maybe they were bedrooms for security or caretakers. It was strange, and certainly unnerving.

Next, he showed me his collection of military tanks and Rolls-Royce cars, including one that he claimed had belonged to Eva Braun, Hitler's wife. Then he said to me I could take it back to Malibu with me. He brought me to another room that housed a massive collection of knives, axes, and other weapons. He took my hand gently and pulled me to a spot behind a line. He chalked my hands . . . and I found myself throwing knives. From four meters, then six, then eight. I guess I have very good aim, he seemed pleased. I explained lightly that it must have been all the training I endured for a silly movie called *Barb Wire*. I laughed at that but was met with silence. At that point, I turned to my companion for support, but he just looked down, uncomfortable. I said I was tired. I thought it might be time to leave.

He walked me out to our car, where the rest of the team was waiting for us. I thanked him and said I'd be in touch. He gave me his number—and a set of ninja throwing stars as a parting gift. I'm not sure if he ever made the donation to IFAW, but I still keep the throwing stars in a dresser, next to my bed.

MY FRIENDSHIP WITH JULIAN ASSANGE HAS BEEN INVIGORATING, sexy, and funny. Though his circumstances are not funny at all. Ten years incarcerated, in one way or another. We were first introduced through Vivienne Westwood. I visited Julian regularly at the Ecuadorian embassy in London, staying for hours at a time. He looked forward to the vegan meals I'd bring him, and he was intrigued by my perspective on global issues. Most of his visitors were lawyers, politicians, and people he worked with closely on legal matters. My presence was different, maybe, a little refreshing, human. Somewhat stimulating for him. I brought with me another world, one that wasn't so heavy.

Through our colorful conversations, Julian taught me so much about the world. He reminded me a lot of my grandpa in that way. Julian would draw diagrams about any topic and loved to solve problems, no matter how small or how large. It could be a conversation about jealousy—*Is there a rival?* he'd ask—or why people keep changing up the Bible, or how to stay safe on the Internet by closing all its doors. Julian believed in saving people by offering truth and education: if wars are started by lies, truth can end them. He was bringing to light secrets and corruption in governments, and now he's paying the price for all of us. His idea was that we must stay true to ourselves and the planet, and never stray from our principles. We must support one another when we are brave enough to use our skill set at its highest value, and do all we can to keep each other safe. Even though, inevitably, some risk their lives more than others do.

I feel like we have really let Julian down, so far.

One night, Julian and I shared a strong bottle of mezcal. We passed out, and I woke up at four in the morning with his cat on my chest. We'd both fallen asleep following a slightly frisky, fun, alcohol-induced night together. My car was still waiting outside, and I'm sure that sent some tongues wagging. We joked about getting hitched on the front steps of the embassy—maybe then they wouldn't arrest him? But then again, he joked, why would he give up one prison for another? His sense of humor— funny in an uncanny way and so alarmingly smart—made me think of some friends and family with similar quirks of brilliance and social awkwardness. They didn't know what to do with their unique minds. Many I know resorted to drinking, computer games, or crossword puzzles. I'm sure that's the way of a lot of bright people, not wanting to follow the herd, confused because their intuitions and instincts are telling them to do something different.

Conflicted feelings
are to be examined closely

but it is often easier to stay numb—
and not do the work—
Earth,
gravity,
miracles take longer.

By his request, I was the first person to visit Julian at Belmarsh, the supermax prison. It was a shocking experience—the five checkpoints, the shouting and screaming while we crossed through the yard. We had gone in a different, more secure way, so as not to be exposed to the general population. That was the prison's call, the safest way, they said, for me and for the inmates. It was the most frightening place I've ever visited. Julian is a mild-mannered person, not a physical threat to anyone, and he is being broken down, psychologically tortured. He doesn't belong there.

I tried to find more clever ways to help my friend, to bring attention to Julian's wrongful incarceration. I engaged in a variety of public-facing missions. I took a job doing a commercial in Australia as an excuse to go to the country and meet Julian's mom, Christine. She came to my hotel room and met me with a warm embrace, a strong hugger, just like her son. I had brought with me the cash resources she needed, as a donation, which she used to help send two MPs from Parliament to visit Julian in jail. She's such a bighearted woman, so engaged in the world, and so distraught over her son. Christine is a brilliant woman and a straight shooter. She was quick to give me advice about my life and career. She said she'd spoken to Julian about me, and she knew I deserved a lot more respect than people gave me, especially in the media. But it was partly my own fault, she pointed out, because of the way I had utilized my image. She told me to stop posting sexy photos on social media, to post authentic ones, ones with my sons or pets, with less makeup, not retouched. She thought that it would help me become a stronger and more serious activist, because my intelligence was being overshadowed. I was touched by her sentiment and concern, appreciated her advice, and took it under serious consideration.

But, I argued, I am who I am, which is a combination of all I know, and I've always believed that striving to be a sensual person, or being sexy, should not conflict with intelligence. Women have fought hard so that we do not need to limit ourselves. And this confirmed for me that I had to use all I had even more to get attention for what was right. If the cartoon image of me was what got me through the door, so be it. And so I continued the work the only way I knew how. It was too late to turn back now, I thought—it would take time and effort to try to change people's opinion of me. Still, I kept her challenge at the back of my mind.

While I was in Australia, I had hoped to meet with PM Scott Morrison, to make a plea in person to the Australian government to help Julian, a brave citizen whom the country should be so proud of. The smear campaign and propaganda directed at him were immense; people didn't even know why they didn't like Julian—they just didn't, they fell for it. After I wrote an open letter to Mr. Morrison, he responded cheekily in the press by saying he'd love to meet me, if he could bring a few of his buddies along. That didn't go over well—women were unimpressed with his insensitive remarks, which, by then, had reached the international press. Australia and many countries are so indebted to the United States (or afraid of it) that they wouldn't dare do anything against it. It's more complex than that, obviously, but that's the bottom line. Unfortunately, the world is set up this way. I wish we could expand our flexibility without being so emotionally charged.

I understand more and more how the world works
As time passes.
Good and bad.
But I know Julian Assange is a hero.
He will be free one day.
I have to believe that.

XV

To be nobody-but-yourself—in a world which is doing its best,
night and day, to make you everybody else—means to fight
the hardest battle which any human being can fight; and
never stop fighting.

—E. E. CUMMINGS

(the quote I put in both boys' graduating yearbooks)

My biggest loves
of all
are of course my children.
Always,
In every minute,
My beautiful boys
radiate in my heart,
my mind,
my soul.
Bravely making their way
through the life they have been dealt:
Full of empathy and wonder.

When I was away from them,
I would practice a kind of telepathy—
Healing from afar.
I would imagine
a white light surrounding them—
Tracing the images
I held of them in my mind
protecting them, healing them
with loving thoughts
while they slept.
No matter where I was—
I would tell them
We were
a magic triangle—
The three of us always together
No space or time—

They know
They are loved,
and respected . . .

MY KIDS GREW UP IN A WILD WORLD AND HAVE NAVIGATED ITS ups and downs brilliantly. I would tell them, *Happy is only one emotion. All the other feelings are just as important, even sad, even yearning, surprised, disappointed.* I promised them that when they were upset or heartbroken, they would feel joy again, but that they must first sit with those difficult feelings—don't hide from them. Accept them, relish them, then let them go. Honor them. To an artist, an actor, a musician, those feelings are gifts. They're where art is born. They can be uncomfortable minutes, hours, days, but they will pass. To not fear feelings is a great thing to learn—a skill, a practice. We all have our own computer in our brain, and no one can tell anyone else how theirs works. We must find our own self-soothing techniques—mantras, meditation, movement—and embrace them in times of difficulty.

Inspiration cannot be diluted,
Or hidden from
for long.

In order to grow
to create
we have to love—and live—
the questions.

In his *Letters to a Young Poet*, Rainer Maria Rilke says:

You are so young, so much before all beginning, and I would like
to beg you to have patience with everything unresolved in your heart
and to try to love the questions themselves as if they were locked
rooms or books written in a very foreign language. Don't search for
the answers, which could not be given to you now, because you would
not be able to live them. And the point is, to live everything. Live
the questions now. Perhaps then, someday far in the future, you will
gradually, without even noticing it, live your way into the answer.

Growing up, I was always full of questions. I knew I was embarking on a journey, a mysterious life given to me so that I could be the explorer of new thoughts. Living was an action, a currency, and it was up to me how I spent it.

I had an ancient but also free-spirited parenting style. Even though we live in a modern society, it was important to me to think primitively, using the ideas I had learned from my eclectic reading and research alongside the principles of human nature imprinted on us for generations. A modern mythology. When the boys were babies, I wore them in slings, close to my heart. When they were toddlers, I tried to never helicopter-parent, no matter how much I wanted to sometimes. I let them learn to depend on themselves and each other, helping them build survival instincts.

Education was always an important consideration for me . . . Tommy and I agreed it was up to us to lead the horses to water. For kindergarten, our boys went to a Waldorf school, carrying little picnic baskets of fruit and veggies and cloth napkins. They learned to make soup and played with wooden toys. This style of education was created to nurture the spirit of each child, to preserve the imagination, and to end war. Creating a space without competition or capitalism. The boys·went to public school for their elementary years—Malibu is fortunate enough to have great schools.

I also felt it was important that my kids be educated by and about the broader world. I always took them to art galleries, museums, lectures. Even though sometimes they'd rather have been surfing. I felt it was important to expose them to activism and art early on. For Mother's Day every year, I would ask them to take me to the Getty Villa—we loved to walk the museum, full of medieval art, coins, jewelry, sculpture, and magnificent gardens. For my birthday, I asked that we volunteer at the California Wildlife Center, cleaning birdcages and feeding hummingbirds with an eyedropper. We made individual meals for rescued squirrels and once took home a rogue possum that was rehabilitated enough to be set free. Since possums are nocturnal, we waited until dusk, then released him in the same spot where he was found. A fond memory. Imprinting a natural kindness.

We've released rehabilitated pelicans and seals that have survived their circumstances out to the ocean. The boys and I even took a marine mammal rescue course together, just to know what to do in case we came across seals or sea lions on the beach and how to tell whether they were abandoned and in need of nurturing. They were a common sight where we lived. We learned, first of all, not to go near them—the mom was probably hunting nearby—and to just keep an eye out and call the professionals in if they looked skinny or had been left alone too long. These types of bonding experiences were so special.

WHEN I WAS A BABE IN LADYSMITH, THE ATKINSON BOYS WENT TO Shawnigan Lake School, a world-renowned boarding school on the island. I was always curious about this mysterious, magical place. It was an all-boys school, with huge Tudor-style buildings among hundreds of manicured acres. I told myself if ever I were to have boys, I wanted them to go there.

And so when the time came to consider where to send them for high school, Shawnigan was the place. The academics were rigorous, and the school's take on discipline was forward-thinking—consequences for antics and pranks were seen as teachable moments. It felt like the right kind of school to help my boys to grow into the men they were meant to be.

A dream realized.

Brandon went beginning in eighth grade, a year ahead of Dylan. He was nervous, understandably—though Shawnigan was close to our family property and to his grandparents, it was far away from his idyllic Malibu lifestyle. Dropping him off was so hard, but I knew it was an important moment for both of us. Before the boys were born, I read *The Continuum Concept* by Jean Liedloff, about attachment parenting and how if children's needs are always met early on, they will grow up secure and confident and form healthy attachments later in life. It was enlightening—in it, she writes about children born to Indigenous people, how to trust that your children are safe, to have faith in them through all the stages of life. I was moved by her description of an aboriginal rite of passage, where a mother walks her thirteen-year-old son onto a bridge, a cruel but poignant ceremony. The mother leads him to the center of the bridge, then turns and walks away without looking back. The ceremony is acted out with screams and cries from the child and a fierce, stoic sense of confidence and pretended disregard from the mother. Liedloff stressed how important it is for boys to detach at this age, to move forward on their own road, so they can mature and form new relationships.

I kept this in mind as we headed to the first day of school. I knew I had to be strong. We stood eye to eye on the sidewalk, holding hands. I told Brandon he was going to be okay as he stared into my soul for reassurance, then I had to drive away and leave him there with his little suitcase and all he needed for the semester ahead. I watched him in the rearview mirror growing smaller and bigger at the same time. He stood in the driveway, in tears, watching me go till he couldn't see me anymore. It felt primitive, like a knife through my heart. As soon as I turned the corner, I was hysterical and crying hard. I had to pull over and get myself together before I could drive on. But I was so proud we both pushed through.

The myth
The legend
An important milestone

A year later, when it was time for Dylan to go, Brandon had settled in, though he was still homesick from time to time. Dylan was a comfort to Brandon, and they gravitated to one another in this setting. But the school also knew to separate them, if only slightly; they lived in the same "house," but on different floors with other roommates, who became, by a stroke of luck, lifelong friends. And if they were too homesick, their grandparents were only an hour away. My mom would bring them cookies, apple pies, her famous Nanaimo bars—they looked forward to her coming by with treats for everyone.

My parents were always amazing grandparents, lifesavers. Impressively, they stuck it out together over the years, and they are now even more madly in love, inseparable. One is lost without the other.

A lesson, learning, discovering.

The kind of love that's wounded
But pure
Admittedly courageous
Only slightly more mature.

When the kids were babies, my dad would take them for walks in their strollers to spend some one-on-one time with them in nature. He would explain all sorts of things about the universe to them, from plants to trees to animals to insects. He loved conversing with the boys—I think he felt freer talking to them than he did with some adults. They were worth his while.

My dad was never a social person, especially in his later years. I suspect he felt children were smarter than adults—definitely a more captive audience—and he was right. He loved the innocent banter, the wide-eyed questioning, and especially the un-thought-out truths that came from them. It's hard to find that kind of authenticity. The way he was with my sons reminds me of how Grandpa Herman was with me. Grandpa was hard on my dad but was gentle and kind with me and could talk to me about anything. I appreciated my grandfather in a different way, without judgment. I was a fresh slate to him. The cycle continues.

I traveled a lot for work when the boys were at Shawnigan, but my schedule was based around their school year. I visited as much as I could, and they came home to Malibu around once a month, and for holidays and summers, of course. Still, it was hard on us. It hurt to send them back, and they didn't always want to go. I knew my kids needed consistency and structure, and Shawnigan would supply them with the positive male role models that they were missing and a good Canadian education: grounded, with manners. I'm sure I survived LA only because of my Vancouver Island roots. I knew with all my heart that my boys needed to be on the island in their formative years to survive the years ahead.

Both boys thrived at Shawnigan. Dylan was prefect of his graduating year. His peers looked up to him and came to him for advice, tutoring, or consultation. He loved music and songwriting, and his solo guitar performances were something everyone looked forward to. That adulation gave him courage and confidence in his natural abilities as an artist. Brandon was involved in the theater, a stunningly hilarious Lord Farquaad in *Shrek*, to standing ovations. When he graduated, Brandon received the prestigious Performing Arts Award, or, as he likes to say, "the high school equivalent of a Tony."

At Shawnigan, the boys found what they were naturally good at. Their callings—or, at least, their beginnings. Now they both assure me they will one day send their kids to Shawnigan and they both thank me for making that difficult decision and sticking to it—with love—even when there were tears and foot-stomping defiance.

Some kids don't get the challenges they need to persevere, while others, sadly, are given too many. Brandon and Dylan are true miracles, considering the gene pool. They are well-adjusted and confident, they don't hide from intimacy, they are romantics, they are willing to take risks. They have been through so much, yet they are not full of holes. My philosophy about parenting has proven true.

In the tradition of Kahlil Gibran, I wanted to be "the bow."

You are the bows from which your children
As living arrows are sent forth
The archer sees the mark upon the path of the infinite
And he bends you with his might

That his arrows may go swift and far
Let your bending in the archer's hand be for gladness
—"ON CHILDREN," KAHLIL GIBRAN

After they graduated from Shawnigan, we encouraged the boys to pursue a college education. Dylan was accepted to USC for music and neuroscience (he is a math whiz, and math is music), though Tommy and I were no help at all. Dylan had audited a few classes at USC with his father about the music business, and Tommy fell asleep in the class and started snoring.

But both boys felt like they didn't fit into traditional universities, so they left during their first semesters. They wanted to get on with it. It didn't come without consequence—Tommy and I told them if they left school, they were on their own. Our kids were responsible for their choices at this point—we were there for them, but not to support them financially if they made the tough decision to not stay in school. They understood they had to weigh the consequences.

After sleeping on a friend's couch, Brandon got a job making smoothies at SunLife Organics in Malibu and then pursued his passion part-time. He decided to take acting classes geared to support what he imagined his future could be. Brandon also has an intuitive mind for business and explored options in that realm. One summer, he interned in Brazil for a São Paulo ad agency. Brandon stayed with our friend Guga and his wife, learning a little Portuguese, and helped to create ad campaigns for Red Bull and Nike.

Dylan had left USC after seeing too many weekend ambulances carry off young people who'd partied too hard, overdosed. He hated the fraternity culture, he didn't fit in and had seen enough. So he went on to pursue his interest in music elsewhere, auditioning and getting accepted to a music school more suited to his artistic wants, style, and ambitions. He also had an interest in finance, interning for a summer in New York at the stock exchange. He went with Conrad, his surf buddy from Malibu, who is like family to us. The two of them went to H&M and bought a few suits in different colors, which they shared on alternate days at BGC Partners. While they learned a lot, they also learned they definitely didn't want to be stockbrokers. But they were inspired by cryptocurrencies, blockchain, and international finance, which influenced both of their careers.

At twenty years old, Brandon shocked us all by asking if he could take what remained of his college fund and use it to go to rehab. He wasn't in any trouble, but he was starting to experiment and realized he might have that thing that ruins people's lives. He had seen too much of it in his young life and wanted nothing to do with it. Brandon made a proactive decision, probably the best of his life. He wanted to do it on his own, not because he had to, but because he wanted to understand who he was. He knew he was genetically loaded and was smart enough to understand what that meant. There, they gave him a fresh start and tools to navigate temptation. It was just what he needed to remove the roadblocks he brilliantly foresaw. He would pursue his dreams as an artist, an actor, with so much to draw upon, levels of life and emotion. The fact that he chose to do this still amazes me—it wasn't the easy way. Tommy, Dylan, and I participated in the family program, and it brought us all closer as we talked out the circumstances of our family history and tendencies.

My children blow my mind every day. They are not entitled, they are hardworking, serious. Dylan is extremely sensitive and profound. He internalizes his feelings, yet they appear in his music, and he remains a private person. He is a sleeper, a big-picture guy. I watch him with curiosity—he's onto something.

As for Brandon, he is a wizard. I like to call him a financial artist. Nobody knows what this boy is capable of yet, not even him.

Through wise strategy and cutting-edge investments in the arts, Brandon and Dylan made enough money to buy a home together in Malibu. They complement each other and enjoy living together. And they both have such style. I remember one time when they were young teenagers, I took the boys to the Hammer Museum's exhibition *Between Earth and Heaven: The Architecture of John Lautner,* which left an impression. It's been so rewarding to see how the boys developed their sense of style: warm minimalism, midcentury, case-study homes. Sustainability. Blending their home into the natural environment, putting nature first. My boys have great instincts when it comes to architecture and art. Style can't be bought—it's a sixth sense, an instinct. They've got it.

> *It's always a challenge to create something new,*
> *to be a pioneer—*
> *and many don't care enough*
> *to allow their minds to wander*
>
> *There is always a "formula,"*
> *the quick fix*
> *to achieve something.*
> *How boring.*

Joseph Campbell had great advice
To never follow the bewildered herd.
I agree.
Forge a new path—
It takes courage, vision, and faith
In one's self.
To be successful is very hard work.
Luck is earned.

XVI

I'm restless.
Things are calling me away.
My hair is being pulled by the stars again.
—ANAÏS NIN

I FIRST FELL IN LOVE WITH SAINT-TROPEZ AFTER I SHOT THERE for *Playboy*, around the time of my first film. The colorful buildings, the language . . . the golden light. I noticed with sweet appreciation that everyone had a dog with them, even in restaurants.

When my kids had graduated and settled into the beginnings of their adult lives, I headed back to the Côte d'Azur, a promised pilgrimage. I wasn't sure how long I'd stay—it was an adventure I felt pulled toward. I had to see it through. In an emergency, I could be home in twelve hours. The world condenses in love. We're never too far from one another, anywhere in the world.

I curated my own French style, filling my large Prada trunk with a bounty of treasured things. I flew with my golden retriever, Zou Bisou Bisou (like the song), otherwise called Zeus by my sons and Zuzu by everyone else. I walked barefoot through town, in a little red Bardot-inspired dress, hair teased up at the crown, skipping along the promenade on the water, my woven basket and espadrilles in hand, off to fetch my morning coffee at Sénéquier. Zuzu and I would share an extra-large croissant, with a giant water bowl for him and an espresso with steamed almond milk for me. Zuzu was patient but excited. He knew that just around the corner he would get to take his morning swim at La Ponche. Everyone in the village knew and loved him. *Bonjour, Zuzu!* would ring from the balconies over the striped awnings. The smell of bakeries and the salty sea was not lost on me. I carried a big smile with me everywhere I went.

On afternoons, we'd all go to Club 55—"Cinquante-Cinq"—a dreamy hangout spot with thatch-roofed loungers on the beach. We would sit under the white sailcloth and devour fresh crudité platters of crisp whole vegetables—entire heads of cauliflower, carrots with lacy tops, pleasantly fragrant green onions—piled high like a bouquet on a thick, rustic wood board. An edible centerpiece. Zuzu was always given his own serving of cold, crisp celery—you could hear him crunch throughout the whole restaurant, over the band of guitar players strolling through. We would see many familiar faces there, a glam and clever crowd, and a lot of other dogs were lying cozily under tables.

I'd like to think all the dogs of our past await us in heaven.

I took mandatory Canadian French in school and could read and understand most of it, though in speaking I was shy, only a beginner. I preferred Parisian French and wanted no Quebecois accent. So I immersed myself in a French book I had, Napoleon's love letters to Josephine, to try to absorb its wonderful cadences. I traveled with an assistant, Jeremy, a darling from the South of France. It was a perfect arrangement—he was able to be close to his family, and I could pick up the language from a native speaker. I asked him to speak only French with me. He tried, but it was harder than I thought.

A challenge. The brain twisting. I always desired some sort of misery.

Jeremy and I had similar taste. We both loved the Virgin Mary, aperitifs, and beautiful men. He found the most gorgeous dog nannies for Zuzu, and we swam in all kinds of champagne, like a burlesque dancer splashing playfully in a larger-than-life *coupe de rosé*.

We rented a house in the *centre*. I couldn't have been more thrilled. Occasionally, I'd bump into friends. I'd see Karl Lagerfeld at Sénéquier some mornings, decked out in a pure Chrome Hearts rock-and-roll ensemble. Black leather and dripping in heavy gothic jewelry. He warmly told me that he had his eye on me, that he knew what I was up to, and that he loved it. And to never stop being me. He tenderly touched my face with his biker-gloved hand, then with a serious stare and a naughty smile, he invited me to his next show in Paris. An homage to a girl like me, he said.

Paris was only a few hours away by train. I loved taking the trains in Europe—they were romantic and provided a great opportunity to read. A few chapters of a book, and before you knew it, you would be pulling into Gare du Nord. Karl sat me in the front row of his show. Within the Grand Palais in Paris, he'd created a beach as a runway, complete with lifeguard towers. Wet waves rolled in alongside the models as they walked the sand to a soundtrack of seagulls. It was one of Karl's last shows for Chanel—and it was rightfully dramatic and stunning. We reminisced about the fashion shoot we did together at my house in Malibu, when he brought along his stylist, the beautiful late L'Wren Scott. Karl was just beginning his photography career and asked if he could shoot me in my garden. I agreed but said to please be very low-key—people respected privacy in The Colony. I asked that he bring as few people as possible, so imagine my shock and surprise when two huge semitrucks full of clothes, shoes, and props arrived, blocking driveways, congesting the tiny street. The back of one truck was open, and the statuesque Ms. Scott was waving to me as they pulled in. Karl said to me he had narrowed it down the best he could. I had to laugh, because he really meant it.

The shoot took only an hour, but getting ready took much longer. Karl would assist the hairdresser, spraying sticky white dry shampoo into my hair, tousling it to new heights. Higher and higher. A neighbor walked by—I think it was Tom Hanks—and asked me, *Is that Karl Lagerfeld in your garage?* I said yes. He chuckled, shook his head, and walked away. It was an honor to work with Karl. A legend, a genius. His passing was a huge loss to the world.

In Saint-Tropez, my two constant companions were Zuzu and a book. I had a suitcase full—I knew I'd get a lot of reading done. I also planned to visit the Colombe d'Or, an old artist colony turned hotel. I wanted to imprint myself with art, retrace the steps of artists like Picasso and Matisse, and read. At a coffee shop on the port, I'd bring the poetry of Jens Peter Jacobsen or Emily Dickinson, opening a book up anywhere, letting it set the tone for the day. I liked the mixed and matched locations, the juxtaposition. Reading of London while on a French terrace. A good way to shake up one's soul at breakfast—a solid habit of mine.

Most sunrises, I'd sit outside basking under the red awnings of Sénéquier, people-watching, gazing at the yachts in the harbor, luxuriating in my own blossoming life. The regulars always caught each other's attention. I instantly gravitated to a charming elderly gentleman named Simon. He sat alone at his table—you could tell it was his ritual. He always had a kind word for me in French I could understand, spoken slowly and clearly. It was not his native language, so we were in the same boat . . . We started to time our coffees together, then Zuzu and I eventually joined him at his table each morning, where we discussed the news of the day from under his stack of newspapers. I eventually found out he was a powerful shipping tycoon. You'd never have known from his laid-back style. I love older gentlemen, with the wisdom that could come only from time on earth. Simon's elegant wife, Joyce, joined us on occasion and shared with me an undeniable empathy and zest for life. Joyce was well-versed in charity, and we bonded over the cares of the world. We had a lot to talk about. They were impressed, and dug my dedication and engagement with the world.

I'd long been involved with refugee organizations, and when I first arrived in France, I took a train to the northern coast, to Calais, where refugees—from Sudan and the African continent, from Kurdish Iraq, from Syria and Afghanistan— lived in the "Calais Jungle" while waiting for asylum. It was a makeshift tent city with insufficient food and water and poor sanitation. Entire families were living there, vulnerable. Choose Love provided assistance with food, clothing, and education, and I was compelled to ask them if I could be of any help, suggesting I could cook healthy vegan meals and read to the children. They said they'd be ecstatic to have me. It was a humbling experience. I brought boxes of much-needed supplies and food, cooking a massive vat of lentil soup. I also handed out children's books to help kids learn French and English, and would read aloud to a wide-eyed audience. I thought Zuzu would bring some joy and comfort, but some of the children, and even the men, were frightened by him—I hadn't realized that dogs were used in horrible ways, to instill fear, in some of the countries they were running from. Eventually, Zeus won them over, and all ended in happy kisses and hugs. Zuzu was so patient, and one young man took his leash and ran around with him, introducing him to others, disappearing for a while into the wooded areas, then returning, to my relief, with even more people petting and playing with him. It seemed healing to me. Zeus is an angel.

My foundation was already working with refugee camps around the Mediterranean. I had noticed that Ai Weiwei, an artist I loved and respected, was creating art installations out of lifeboats and life jackets—heartbreaking work. It inspired me to help raise funds to buy the van they needed at Choose Love. The van was like a rolling phone booth. Its Wi-Fi and electricity gave people a place to use a cell phone and call home, to let loved ones know they were safe. It was a lifeline. We filled the van with baskets of fruit and blankets to hand out. Police were taking away blankets, hoping to get rid of the refugees. When, later, the Calais Jungle caught on fire, people reported that the police just watched it burn.

WE GROW IN ALL DIRECTIONS.

I was searching my way forward, starting to build a meaningful life in France. And while in Paris, I was in my glory. I chose to marinate in Montmartre for a month. I enjoyed the funky architecture and cobbled streets, where I learned to wear flat shoes. I would roam to churches, lighting candles at the Sacré Coeur, and then walk along to my private ballet class. Then I was off to a quirky art class I'd discovered. I was learning to sketch animals from an artist who worked at the natural history museum. She had drawn animals for encyclopedias, and I thought it might be something I'd like to try. It was very detailed work. She taught me to draw using rulers for even the most micro measurements and ratios. I was happiest working with pencil. I visited the Michelangelo exhibit at le Louvre a few times, mesmerized by his drawings, how he used shading to carve out muscle and bone, bodies and body parts emerging on the page. The hands must be the hardest part, I thought.

I was soaking it in, evolving, growing, changing, crystallizing. A chrysalis.

I realized eventually that my walking routine took me past the famous chanteuse Dalida's house, where she sadly committed suicide. I had been listening to Dalida's music and was touched by her "Je suis malade." Shattered, more like it. It shook me to the bone. *I am sick.* (Yes, we are.)

She had left behind a note saying:

La vie m'est insupportable.
Pardonnez-moi.

Life is unbearable to me.
Forgive me.

Her story reminded me how awful celebrity can be, how some women are painfully targeted, and how much it hurts to be exploited. Used and objectified constantly. It can destroy every bit of belief you have in yourself. It is not easy to reconcile the love and admiration you feel from most of the world and the loneliness, abuse, and deceit of some of those closest to you.

You could live and breathe in Paris for a long while without discovering all its tender, secret spots. I searched and found where Anaïs Nin and Henry Miller sat for coffee in Clichy, a less glamorous place than I had imagined. Its day had come and gone—the artists had moved again. But then, Henry's world was rough, rowdy, and raw . . . I walked through the tiny streets and dreamed of their writing and loving together. I have read everything by Anaïs Nin. I especially love her diaries and her erotic short stories. Her imagination and writing style captivated me. I wondered how she protected her lovers and her family, as I feel odd about writing about people in my life. But she was brave and open. She too didn't want to hurt anyone with her words. I feel the same. I dance between protecting everyone and blurting out the truth.

I think some parts are best left unsaid . . .
Leaving it powerless.

Monaco was a place of ridiculous wealth, gold, elegance. I loved the pomp and glamour. I met Prince Albert at a few charity events, and he was always very kind to me. I couldn't help but ask him to stop using animals in the circus—it was his father who loved the circus so much. He was understandably sentimental about it, but I pleaded with him, saying that times had changed.

I'd come to Monaco for a fundraiser, Formula 1 driver Eddie Irvine's event for Race Against Dementia. Checking into my hotel, I met a tall, dark, handsome man. He was very sweet, offering excited compliments when he realized who I was. He introduced himself as a professional soccer player, then proposed we have a drink later in his room. Before I could say anything in English, Jeremy accepted in French—always the naughty instigator, the romantic. A love bug. It seemed innocent enough.

Later, as he leaned in to pour my champagne, I could smell his cologne. I was already quite seduced.

Adil was my lover during my year in France. It ended in betrayal.

Another lesson,
But par for the course.
The truth is unpleasant.
Let's spare the children.

IT WAS A WILD TIME IN EUROPE, BEFORE THE PANDEMIC, BEFORE hyperinflation, before the war in Ukraine. Before it became popular to be "green," drive an electric car, or greenwash, I traveled across the European continent, from Graz and Berlin to Copenhagen and Brussels, pushing for a "Green New Deal" for Europe. The idea was ahead of its time. I met with friend and philosopher Srećko Horvat. Together, we believed we were helping politicians and the public learn about how to face the climate crisis, why building renewable energy sources and investing in public infrastructure was essential. Ideas of how to build a future worth living in. It was a time when everything seemed possible. There is power in collective movements, fighting together with care and love.

I spoke at a few big political events and traveled with activists and comrades, happy to contribute to the dream of Europe and countries around the world existing beyond capitalism. Our message warned that the poor should not be paying for climate change, yet it is the poor who are, once again, paying the highest price.

As my voice became louder in Europe, the same kind of chauvinism and patriarchy I'd encountered elsewhere in the world now came in the form of a guy named Matteo Salvini, a far-right politician who, when I supported refugees, said he "preferred me in costume." I annoyed plenty of people, while also making some true and good forever friends in Europe.

Poetry is a political statement.

I turned to activism and poetry when I was hurting, to express myself, and to remind myself who I was. It helped me tremendously to be busy doing what I felt was meaningful. I wasn't sure how many times a heart could be broken. I guess as many times as it takes.

XVII

When I ache—
I write—
and when I have a muse
I can't write fast enough.
A waterfall—
I can't keep up—
My best words are the forgotten ones . . .

I know when I am being controlled.
I sometimes let it happen,
but it doesn't last long.
Still, we treat ourselves only as well
As we think we deserve.
How we think of ourselves

Brings us down in unclear moments,
but I know myself,
the essence.

THE BOYS AND I DECIDED IT WAS TIME TO PUT THE COLONY house on the market. It sold quickly, breaking price-per-square-foot records. It was beautiful—my masterpiece—sustainable teak and glass, the jewelry of the beach. Every ounce of my career, any money I made, had gone into that house. It was a great investment. Yet in the moment, an eternal money pit. When it sold, I felt a kind of bittersweet relief. Twenty years of hard work and vision paid off. Who would've thought. It was like a savings account, as unconventional as that might sound. A true blessing that has now set me up for the rest of my life. And I am expensive.

As a creator and builder—
I care deeply about
The lines.
Like a body—
The beautiful imperfections,
The weathered spots,
A promise
A handshake.
I've never felt driven by money—
yet—
Somehow, I stay above water
"I am provided for"
is my mantra.

Pure trust.

It was time to go home . . .

XVIII

Ladysmith—
My collection
of sea glass,
exotic hummingbird feeders,
A simple potting shed.
A little chaos—
an
art deco
landscape
shaped by wind.

My funk records
Spinning
Parliament and
Freddie King—

Grooving to
Nina Simone—
singing with her
like no one's there,

(because no one's there)
A kind of freedom—
with reckless abandon—
I holler out—
hitting that note,
"My name is Peaches . . ."

Award-winning family recipes
(can't beat our dill pickles and
homemade mustards),
A forage of
beets, potatoes,
and soon-to-be-stuffed cabbage from
my garden.

I CLIMB THE STEEP SLOPE THROUGH THE GARDEN GATES ONCE again. (That doesn't get any easier.) My arms are weighed by heavy tin buckets overflowing with lettuces, cucamelons, zucchini, and pumpkin flowers ready for their warm vegan ricotta. Heirloom tomatoes await my famous French tarts, which I learned to make in the south of France. The sting of herbs so fresh that when touched, they scent your fingers and bite your nose, tempting a sneeze.

Walking barefoot through my garden, I feel free. Silhouetted in sheer white linen, a lilac sunrise bursting from the ocean behind me. A veil of silence, except for the laughter of swallows, who have stolen the woodpeckers' holes. The water's gentle lapping against the beach house at high tide.

The aching smell
of breakfast calling—
A freshly baked rhubarb pie—
A tiny "centennial rose" teacup—
from my collection
of mismatched china,
A strong espresso
with a drop of oat milk—

Staring into the velvet
ocean.

A mist of imperfect thoughts and dreams. This is my sanctuary. I'm blessed.

My Garden of Eden—
Though not to be cast out—
held captive, maybe—
A safety net—
overcoming false views—
A lifetime to purge,
shedding an old skin—
Reflecting intensely
On my life and loves.
Otters playing,
Henry the heron's tai chi mastery
While
Bald eagles and
Great horned owls

hunt from above
soaring . . .
To a place of rest
perched atop the
decaying dock's piles.

Other than a few annoying clam diggers, this might be paradise.

LIVING ON VANCOUVER ISLAND, YOU CAN'T MISTAKE THE BLEND of scents. The Salish Sea's distinct salty, earthy fragrance, mingled with the wet wood of log booms and boats. My ranch on the water is a vortex, pot-stirring, volcanic, a powerful healing energy. It brings everything to the surface; you can't help but be inspired. And dream vividly.

White heat—
As I lay in the grass—
looking at the stars,
Connecting the dots—
Remembering the names of constellations
Hercules
Orion's belt
Cassiopeia.
Waiting for shooting stars

I feel the energy beneath me
There is something clearly special
Deep below the surface

I imagine
A pyramid—
A crystal glacier—
Something radiates
Magnetic
Elemental—
Deserving of respect

Re-wilding is an amazing concept, to complement the natural landscape and to protect what is already there. On the property, I've incorporated a sustainable water management system and solar energy, and planted clover fields for better water absorption, with no pesticides. Also, a rain-catching experiment of used oak wine barrels with hand pumps connected to gutters on every building. Everything I can do to sustain the property for decades to come—climate change is only getting worse, and investing in sustainable practices is going to ensure that my family can enjoy this place a little longer.

I imagine my grandparents watching all of this. I feel they are still here listening, watching and protecting me.

The softest leaves like honey melt
The sound of knocking heads
A woodpecker's drumbeat
We live in the birds' house—
A fig wasp's final farewell.

My first garden, five thousand square feet of roses and vegetables—a miracle, a metaphor. I planted every seed myself. Everything grew, like, really grew, more than in a normal garden.

Magical seeds? I've wondered. Like in Jack's garden in "Jack and the Beanstalk," my pumpkins and watermelons crawled through the deer fence, hanging like monster orbs. A wild goddess energy here. *Syncretism.* A statue of Kuan Yin, the goddess of compassion, sits meaningfully on my desk.

There are multiple layers to a free spirit. It's not just about being aimless and mindless—it's a pure connection, it's flow. It's an adventure. Intelligence doesn't look like any one thing. It's a best-kept secret, it's mysterious. For me, it's *Singing from the Well* by Reinaldo Arenas, it's the author Nicolas Bouvier's *The Way of the World,* it's Frida's *Self-Portrait with Cropped Hair,* her painful world with Diego, it's Virginia Woolf's poignant *A Room of One's Own,* it's the integrity of Black Panther Angela Davis, it's the jazzy cadence of Kerouac's *On the Road,* it's James Baldwin's deep love theory or Noam Chomsky's far-out lectures. An endless evolution.

XIX

To discover who we are not
Is also a valuable exercise
And I'm grateful to all my teachers
For the strength it takes.
And it takes a lot.

My imagination has been my savior.
An assimilation of feelings
Lived
Dreamt
Or fantasized—
It all leaves a mark

I still bring myself
To places of madness and destruction.
All is lost in love and war.

IT STARTED WITH A ROAD TRIP TO CLEAR MY HEAD. A METAPHOR.
A forward action.

Men are my downfall. And I've tried all kinds. The common denominator is me. I realize I'm only at war with myself when it comes to love.

It was very early in the morning, snow falling hard. I had my trusty assistant Jonathan ready at the wheel. I had taken only a basket of my favorite sweaters and silk pajamas and grabbed a bag of dog food and my protector Zuzu. I knew I had to cocoon. Reprogram. And get back on my own path. Escaping the lies.

I left him to face his own demons as I journeyed on to face my own. Osho's great expression, *The capacity to be alone is the capacity to love,* is a hard one to grasp. But so true.

The road trip was profound. Leaving on the ferry, I looked out the window to a pod of killer whales swimming next to us. You could barely make them out in the fog—majestic, magnificent creatures. A sign. We were driving from Ladysmith to Malibu to visit my sons. It would take three days. I made the most of it, the gasoline was surely tears.

Driving by Mount Shasta, its volcanic and alien energy felt nourishing. A life force. Jonathan was a saint, patiently listening to all my crazy books on tape blasting through the car speakers. He was in therapy, too, whether he liked it or not, while we drove the ten-hour stretches each day. Learning all we could from *Women Who Love Too Much* by Robin Norwood (it should be *People Who Love Too Much*) and the classic *Codependent No More* by Melody Beattie, with Proust and *Leaves of Grass* by Walt Whitman for relief. I'd read these books before, but audiobooks are a different experience, and I let the words wash over me. It was time for some good old-fashioned self-reflection. The idea of writing a book became a real option. I needed something to pour my heart into.

The trip flew by. Stopping in Carmel, a place I love to wander through. Right next to Kerouac's Big Sur. We stopped at Henry Miller's museum and bookstore, picking books in plastic sleeves hanging from trees. Then passed the Esalen Institute, an old nudist colony and a Beat Generation writer hangout. A mountain town surrounded by crashing waves. I resonated with a stormy sea.

Electric
The San Andreas Fault line is my home—
I live along a bumpy and volcanic earthquake zone—
A severe energy
A continental fault
that rides the west coast.

It was a relief to see the Pacific Coast Highway. Dolphins jumping to greet us. A totem.

Just as you enter Malibu, there are huge sand hills to the left and an angry ocean pounding to the right. My friends and I had walked there years before, and my body was yearning to move. Kinetic energy, trapped. So we pulled over. I looked at the hills I used to be able to run up and down time after time. But it was so difficult to do so now. Difficult to breathe—the sand was deep, and my legs ached. I realized how out of shape I was—I hardly recognized myself. I had let myself go.

When I arrived at the boys' house in the hills of Malibu on Las Flores, we were all greeted with warm hugs. Dinosaur, their beloved pit bull, loved Zuzu and remembered him from our last visit. I remember kissing everyone hello and good night at the same time, so exhausted—mind, body, and soul. I crawled right into bed. I was with the people I loved, I reminded myself. I was safe.

Languid, I dreamed of the cat again—my arms stretched out, furry and spotted. A puma with her claws out. Ready to pounce. I was hiding, hunted. Lost and hungry in the jungle.

This was a period of regrowth. I took a month to just reconnect with my boys, Malibu, and nature. Like in years past, I walked the trails around Pepperdine and went to my old Pilates studio. I was determined to connect to my body again—it felt so far away. Secret layers.

With my daily five-mile walks and getting back to my healthy habits, I was detoxing both emotionally and physically. I had to get back on track, yet I had no idea what I was preparing for. The biggest challenge of my career was looming just over the horizon.

The boys and I cooked together, as normal, and watched *RuPaul's Drag Race*—I was honored to be a celebrity guest host, in the fourth season, episode eight. After everyone went to sleep, I'd curl up on my bed and watch inspiring documentaries, short films, ballets, operas, and my favorite directors. The Criterion Channel is a favorite—Fellini's *8½,* anything Jim Jarmusch. One evening, I was scrolling through my phone to view streaming apps, something I'm not good at. Then I fell upon the *Fosse/Verdon* series. I was hooked, binge-watching. I had known so much about these legendary characters, and it was just what I needed. I searched for dances by Fosse and

Verdon and drank it all in. I was dousing myself, annihilating reality, or so I thought.

Hard to believe, but it's true . . . Right at the part where Gwen Verdon is trying to convince Bob Fosse to do *Chicago* on Broadway, I received a message from Barry Weissler, the notable producer of *Chicago* on Broadway. Barry had told a mutual friend, *She needs to come to New York. She IS Roxie Hart. Let's show the world what she's capable of. I'm ready for her, whatever it takes—it's time. Have her call me.*

I almost fell over, convinced I'd manifested it all. I ran downstairs and told the boys. They were delighted, told me, *You have to do it, Mom! You can do this.* Somehow I knew I could do it, too. I needed to do it for my soul—I was ready to take on something of this magnitude, had been preparing my whole life for this. I had nothing to lose.

I called Barry excitedly and said, *Okay . . . I'll do it,* then asked, *When do you think?* imagining he'd say maybe in a year or so. He said, *NOW.*

So Jonathan and I headed by car back to Canada. I had to get Zuzu safely back home, we'd been gone over a month already. Then I'd be turning around in just a few days, and this time I'd fly to LA from Vancouver to start rehearsals. Everything moved so fast. No time to overthink. It was in motion . . . I was going to be on Broadway. I was afraid, burning, a frenzied feeling, manic. I was all over the place.

My mom and dad moved onto my property in Canada finally. It was my evil plan all along to be closer to them in their twilight years. And they loved taking care of my animals, so it was good timing. I headed to LA knowing all were okay, arriving clear-headed to two weeks of insane rehearsals at 3rd Street Dance. Then to New York for another month of next-level preparations before my eight-week run. It was a grinding schedule, eight shows a week, but I was determined. If I was going to do this, it wasn't going to be watered down.

If others could do it, so could I. I just knew I needed to work hard. I may not have been blessed with much natural talent—a lot of people have it—but it's work ethic that separates people. Artists or athletes.

I felt ready—

Roxie had come up once before. About ten years prior, I had been standing on the beach in Malibu, barefoot, with two surfboards under my arms, a trucker hat on a mess of hair, a small cooler swinging painfully from my wrist, impatiently waiting for the boys to say bye to their surf buddies after their surf contest. I was ready to go home and get the day of wind and sand off me when a man approached. I wasn't in the best mood when he introduced himself as Rob Marshall, and he explained he had directed the movie *Chicago*. I still didn't understand why he was telling me this. Then he asked if I'd ever consider being on Broadway. I was taken aback—he was talking . . . to me? Was there someone behind me that this was meant for?

He said that he had been watching me. That he was a musical director and he knew there was very little vulnerability left in Hollywood, and he wished he'd met me sooner. He said he was onto me. He told me that he and his partner were obsessed with me when they saw my rumba on *Dancing with the Stars*—

ironically, a role I took only because it was Auntie Vie's favorite show. He was curious about the characterization I applied to my dances. That stuck with me—I wasn't even sure people noticed that I had put that kind of work into it. It was my secret experiment. The lyrics, a monologue. Still, his suggestion felt so crazy, I just laughed it off. He asked for my number, and I gave it to him in disbelief.

My boys finally came up and were now impatient with me to get to the car—*Mom, Mom, Mom*. Mr. Marshall followed us to the truck. He helped us load the surfboards, then he looked at me and said, *Mr. Weissler is going to call you.*

Barry Weissler, the producer of *Chicago* on Broadway, called the next day. He wanted to meet me at the Beverly Hills Hotel. I love the Beverly Hills Hotel—all good things start there. He offered me "the part" over fancy pink lemonades, but I had no idea what that meant. *Roxie,* he said. And while they worked out the contracts, he wanted me in the studio. I worked some choreography with Greg Butler, I started voice lessons with Eric Vetro . . . but New York? My kids were just starting school up in Canada, it was Dylan's first year. I just couldn't go that far away, knowing that the boys were still adjusting to Shawnigan. When the time came to sign on the dotted line, I had to say no. My boys needed me close by. I couldn't give the show the focus. But I promised I would do it, maybe another time. Barry understood—he had a ton of talent waiting to do it, it didn't set him back. My reasons for not doing it were honorable ones, my kids came first, and the universe ended up validating that good decision by bringing the opportunity back around.

I was in a better place. I had even more of a rich lifetime to draw from. It was time.

BROADWAY WAS THE BEST MEDICINE, A GODSEND. I'VE NEVER worked at anything so hard. Hours of dance, acting, and voice lessons in both LA and New York. The New York team dance captain David Bushman, voice coach Joan Lader, musical director Rob Bowman, piano player Scott Cady, and stage manager David Hyslop became my family. They were not going to let me fail. And they were just as surprised as I was at how hard I was willing to work.

I put all I was feeling into the role—all the heartbreak, the hurt, the trauma. Ivana Chubbuck's *The Power of the Actor* came in handy.

I am the hero of my own story.
And I would play Roxie the same way.
Like no other.
We were aligned, our stories were eerily similar.
We were going to get through this together.

I fell into the rhythms of New York City. It was springtime and Central Park was in bloom—tulips, then daffodils, then peonies. I found refuge in the park's dreamed-up and carefully designed gardens, a system of grids, horse trails, and man-made ponds and fountains—the heart of the city. It became my sanctuary. I walked every day in the park at eight A.M. and it grounded me. I missed my Zuzu, but seeing the dogs in Central Park made me happy. I even found a dog to walk while I was there—a beautiful red Irish setter named Dash that I'd pick up each day on the way to the park, to his busy parents' delight.

Then, after a good walk that included a trip through Strawberry Fields, continued right by the doorway where John Lennon was shot, and headed down the street Gwen Verdon and Bob Fosse's first apartment was on, Central Park West. I'd sit on a bench, look up to their penthouse's stained glass window, and say, *I won't let you down. I won't let you down. I won't let you down.*

A single photo on my dressing room mirror. A picture of me at five years old.

Every night, onstage in front of everyone, the little girl in me was free, the artist, the inevitable child. The pain evaporated opening night, at the first standing ovation. When I was at the theater, I felt safe, and when I was onstage, even safer.

We are made of music
When hope is shattered,
We can be redeemed

I stepped across the threshold of the Ambassador Theatre, appreciating the ornate Beaux Arts architecture, inspired. The theater's chairs were purple velvet, and a massive crystal chandelier hung in the center. The stage had no props, only a few chairs and the actors—dancers did it all. In true Fosse fashion, the choreography told the story. Broadway is like no other place, the performers are like no other people.

When I was onstage, it was the only time in my life I thought of nothing else. Everything felt right, after long periods of feeling wrong. I was finally in the zone. There are no coincidences. We find our own system, cosmology. The writer, the artist, the child untapped, the pain. It was all a gift.

The show was a success, the reviews were stunning. It was different from anything I'd experienced. For the first time, I felt rooted for—and the fact that I was able to accomplish this commanded a new respect. My kids were amazed and so proud of their mom—it meant a lot to me. They came to the first and last shows and recognized the growth in between. They reveled in the newfound respect people had for me. And that felt good. Even Rick came midway through the run, as a surprise—he said he was sincerely impressed but wasn't shocked. He'd always known I was capable of something great. And he was happy for me.

I conquered myself, with fearlessness, slaying dragons, doubts, and insecurities. I played Roxie not as a victim. Taking a page out of my own playbook.

Gushing
I look around
and am able to digest
where I've come from,
in a whole new light.
A Playmate,
A small-town girl in Hollywood—
and feel proud of myself.
No one else in history has had the same story—
I did it all on my own—
and I did it against the odds.

EPILOGUE

The privilege of a lifetime is being who you are.
—JOSEPH CAMPBELL

I DIDN'T THINK I'D WANT TO SPEND THIS PART OF MY LIFE EX-plaining myself to people. This is just one girl's life, my memories, my experience. This is how I did it. This is my own fable. I can offer only my truth. It would take a lifetime to understand another person. We all have complex, nuanced behaviors that make us who we are, or why we are.

Acceptance is a better way to go.

A delicious assurance.

I'm weird and whimsical—
I communicate
with the trees—
that have known me since birth.
They are my barometer—
My temperature—
Touching the wildness in my heart—
That's born of here—
Where I stand now—

Under blazing comets—
Incarnate.
Heartfelt.
I'm searching still—

Back at my farm, a novice baker covered in flour. A vintage apron, a French rolling pin, and a lot of laughter. Serving homemade pasta drenched in my infamous "dirty rose" tomato sauce with a kick—canned tomatoes with a hot pepper, mixed with rose petals plucked straight from the garden. I still drink out of Grandma's jam jars and eat at picnic tables or on a blanket on the beach, remnants from a childhood.

My fragrant hot-pink roses have exploded, thousands of Yves Piagets blooming to heartbreak. Some roses end up scooped into my tousled updo or tucked behind my ear. They are scattered about the house, spilling out of vintage vessels on tables and toilet tanks.

My dogs include two others, Lucky and Lola. Their protective mastiff personalities shine through, and they are always underfoot, looking eagerly for the parts of veggies that I scrape off the counter onto the floor while cooking. Tough dogs can be vegan.

My chores include seeding wild-bird feeders, while hummingbirds need theirs filled with one-fourth sugar and the rest water, and spiked heavier in the winter. Little birds are messengers, they carry secrets of the dead to the living.

I sit in my white Adirondack chair with my reading glasses and a well-worn book on my lap. Today it's Colette's collection of short stories. I'm at the middle, enjoying her descriptions and playful banter. Reading is my only true friend. And nature. I'm always curious and want to know what nature is trying to teach me. Everything is a clue or a sign. And when I get a visitor, I look it up . . .

> *A message of*
> *Hope*
> *Change*
> *Love*
> *Dragonflies circle me,*
> *a static swarm.*
> *I'm growing past self-created illusions,*
> *That limit growth and change,*
> *A symbol of maturity.*
>
> *My dreams have soundtracks.*
> *I hear Stravinsky's crescendo—*
> *The Rite of Spring . . .*
> *Or jazz, Elevator to the Gallows*
> *Like Jeanne Moreau and*
> *Miles Davis—*
> *Never look back—*
> *There is only beauty ahead,*
> *Salvation . . .*
> *Redemption*
> *Glory*
>
> *Who*
> *am I—*
> *when I'm*
> *alone?*

I'm 5'7"
about 120 lbs

My
eyes
are a sea green
gray
And blue
with a lilac
hue like my dad's—
They
change color with my mood
Our eyes can't hide secrets.

My hair
is naturally platinum now
Pastel honey blond left from
Drugstore box color
Silver at the root
Nature's highlights
strung throughout—

I like it finally—
All the colors of my life
Blending together
An abalone shell—
My hair is still thick and shockingly healthy
After all it's been through
It grows fast (probably from all the vitamins I take)
Underneath the hair
Just a few emotional aches and physical pains—

My mind
is a wanderer
I'm sad a lot.
A poet,
But
I relish the uncharted—
Searching
for the feeling I can't find—
Life's
Sherlock Holmes—

I don't trust anyone,
I trust everything—

I'm hormonal,
moody,
and
silly—

I'm happiest
In my garden—
And when my family visits.
The porch is my altar—
Guarded by a statue of St. Francis.

My roses
waited to bloom—
The first one opened
on the day I got home from New York
I returned gleefully to
Nature's sweet applause

They had
made it through
the abnormally long
wet winter and waited
To welcome me.
To honor me—

Everything
is becoming happier with me home—

I want
to savor these precious moments
being alone with my dogs,
trying my hand at pottery with a wheel and a kiln—
an art studio nestled into the garden

It feels good

And,
Like Monk's House,
Virginia Woolf's garden,
It will all grow in time—

Patience is learned
next—
I will build my writer's cabin
That overlooks the sea
Windows
framed by white fluffy hydrangeas

An old wooden
writing desk

Rooms
of gardens
and music
I will walk
and not talk for days
But I'll never stop
Writing . . .
Creating
Percolating
Loving everything in my path—

A permafrost of emotion
Has been unearthed,
Unknown.

Nothing's impossible it seems.
Evasive only.
You are not alone in this.
Keep searching.
There's always a mountain to climb.

ACKNOWLEDGMENTS

Let's just say this journey has been . . . therapeutic?
Digging my heels in, demanding I write this book myself.
No ghostwriters
no collaborators
or book doctors.
It was like I was screaming inside (and outside)
to just allow me to tell my story
My way—
please—
It really was life or death for me.
I must write my own book,
or I'll die.

The drama . . .

I MUST APOLOGIZE TO AND ALSO THANK THE PEOPLE WHO PUT
up with me. I'm eternally grateful. I had no idea what writing a
book like this would entail—the time, the difficulty, the hyper-
speed learning curve.

I have a newfound respect for the industry. This book started out as a fifty-page poem and then grew into hundreds of pages of . . . more poetry . . . from my first memory to my most recent.

My editor, Kate Napolitano, at HarperCollins is a saint. From our first meeting, I knew she was the one, and after meeting with many publishers, there was no doubt. She fought hardest for this book, and I loved her forward-thinking and up-for-the-challenge attitude. I warned her that I'm not easy, and that only excited her—*The tougher this book is to write, the better it will be.* I couldn't make any promises that we'd agree in the end—and had one foot out the door, wondering if this was a good idea at all. She was true and steadfast, assuring me when I needed it most. Her confidence in me encouraged me to dig deeper and work harder, and her advice came in a cool package of red hair and tattoos. She enjoyed my original writing style, but she also suggested we add full sentences and paragraphs. I told her I don't think in full sentences, let alone paragraphs. The skin on my arms crawled with rage, and I asked, *Why? Why do we need to follow rules?!* Oy. I get it now.

In poetry, there is a lot left to the imagination, but also a raw honesty. Poetry touches the vulnerable spots but doesn't call anyone out. It's poignant but also a shield. I've always written to understand how I feel. I realized I *needed* to do this. I may have turned into the girl in *The Exorcist* a few times—my head spinning, pea soup. I didn't realize how much anger I was holding in Pandora's box. Writing this book was an agonizing task, so much harder than I thought it would be—and, Kate, you managed those times with grace and care. Thank you for your dedication, patience, and pure will to get this done.

Now enter the wonderful Andra Miller. We also had a rough start, but we fought through to the good stuff. Andra, you had the tough job of helping me shape my thoughts in a different way. Your background of editing fiction was crucial, and the admired perspective I needed. I was a mess . . . I broke down many times while you sat there patiently helping to guide me through all the feelings and rabbit holes we went down together. I know I'm stubborn, but it's a survival skill. I'm pleasantly proud in the end—and I wouldn't want this book to be anything other than what it is. A true labor of love. Thank you for all.

I'd also like to thank my writing agents, David Kuhn and Nate Muscato at Aevitas, who had to step in a few times to encourage me; my agent, Chis Smith at APA; my lawyer, Don Steele (our family business's rock); my PR agent and friend, Matt Berritt; and my assistant, Jonathan Zeiler, the glue that holds me together.

My mom and dad deserve my deepest thanks and respect. They have been supportive of me through and through, without hesitation, and taught me everything I know about love.

I am grateful for my brother, Gerry, who has turned over his own new leaf in getting sober and starting fresh. I'm proud of you, G. You are a selfless, committed man, and your wife and children are lucky to have you. Thank you for being my partner in crime from our earliest days together. I am grateful that we reconnected in a healthy way, as we share a lot of the same story.

A special thank-you to my beautiful children, Brandon and Dylan Lee. This was your idea. And I'm truly honored, sweethearts. I was hesitant, but you knew I needed to take back my life story, our story. I can breathe better and move forward now with grace. A new beginning . . .

Brandon, you work so hard. You are a fierce and natural agent, a role you took on with surprise—spontaneously, without fear. And you always make me laugh. *Mom, please write some-*

thing that people can understand. I read your emails, and you sound crazy. Nobody knows what you're talking about! I'm known to ramble, go off on philosophical tangents. I write like I think—but I hope this book makes sense. I think we got the job done.

Dylan, you are the Buddha of the family. Your calmness and musicality are inspiring. The calm in the storm. But I also know you carry a heavy burden—you're an artist, and you feel things deeply. I hope now that this story is out in the world— the truth—you will at least be able to understand a little better why people do what they do. And when we know how people are formed, we can let go of judgment. A chain reaction. We can also celebrate the hard times, as the good times ring even sweeter because of them.

It's no secret. Both of you boys are born from a rare kind of romantic love. Which leads me to Tommy. Thank you for just being you, and for being the catalyst of everything good in my life.

There is no woe-is-me in this book. It is a celebration, a scrapbook of imperfect people living imperfect lives and finding the joy in that. Forgiveness is our salvation. There is redemption in the wisdom that we should never be dependent on others for our own happiness. We cannot save another, we can only love them.

We are the heroes of our own story. It's primitive. We are all monkeys.

Warrior cry. *Memento mori* (remember that you [have to] die).

SELF-PORTRAIT

ABOUT THE AUTHOR

Pamela Anderson is an international icon whose work spans both entertainment and activism. Through the Pamela Anderson Foundation, she champions causes close to her heart, including ocean and rain forest conservation and the protection of vulnerable humans and animals. Above all else, being a mother to sons Brandon Thomas Lee and Dylan Jagger Lee has been Pamela's priority and greatest source of pride.